NAGA IDENTITY

About the Author

B.B. Kumar, M.A. (Hindi), M.Sc. (Chemistry) and M.Sc., Ph.D. (Anthropology), was formerly the Principal of Sao Chang Government College, Tuensang and Science College, Kohima. He was also member of the Executive Council, Academic Council, and University Court of the North-Eastern Hill University.

Dr. Kumar has written/edited/co-authored about 135 books and more than 100 papers. Also, he edited quarterly journal *The Thinker* for 13 years. Presently, he is Editor of the quarterly journals *Dialogue* and *Chintan-Shrijan*.

NAGA IDENTITY

B.B. Kumar

CONCEPT PUBLISHING COMPANY, NEW DELHI-110059

Cataloging in Publication Data—DK
Courtesy: D.K. Agencies (P) Ltd. <docinfo@dkagencies.com>

Kumar, B. B. (Braj Bihari), 1941-
Naga identity / B.B. Kumar.
p. ; cm.
Includes bibliographical references.
Includes index.
ISBN 8180691926

1. Naga (South Asian people)—India. 2. Naga (South Asian people)—India—History. 3. Naga (South Asian people)—India—Politics and government. 4. Nagaland (India)— Politics and government. I. Title.

DDC 305.891 4 21

ISBN 81-8069-192-6

First Published 2005

Published and Printed by
Ashok Kumar Mittal
Concept Publishing Company
A-15/16, Commercial Block, Mohan Garden, New Delhi-110 059

Phones : 25351460, 25351794
Fax : 091-11-25357103
E-mail : publishing@conceptpub.com

Dedicated to
the Memory of
My Father

MAP OF
NAGALAND

FOREWORD

I have great pleasure in putting forward my friend Braj Bihari Kumar's Book *Naga Identity* to the readers. Dr. Kumar is a dedicated scholar and teacher who has lived and worked in the north-east and has brought this book as a labour of love. This book is in the genre of the first account of the Nagas published in English language authored by R.B. Pemberton in 1832 based on his personal experience followed by distinguished scholars and administrators like J.P. Mills, J.H. Hutton, T.C. Hodson, E.A. Gait, Verrier Elwin, S.K. Bhuyan, H.K. Barpujari, N.K. Das, Furer Haimendorf, and scholars and leaders hailing from Nagaland like C.L. Imchen and Hokishe Sema.

To students of history, sociology, politics, administration and religion, the Nagas have invariably invoked both awe and fascination. This feeling is a product of a large variety of imaginations and myths: of the Naga image of 'head-hunters'; of a group of people who would never harm children and women whatever may be the provocation or the need; of their phenomenal attachment to their villages; of their deep sense of humour. This feeling is also shared by all those who have come in contact with the Nagas; be they be Assamese *gossains* or Christian missionaries; civilian administrators or members of the armed forces; travelers or inquisitive visitors; small traders or migrant business houses; road builders or students from neighbourhood.

The Nagas have led a cloistered existence. The process of opening up commenced with the British annexation of Assam in a big way during the nineteenth century led and supported by Christian missionaries. The British encouraged Christian missionaries to play a major role in the entire north-eastern region including Nagaland. Accordingly, various missionary groups hailing from U.S.A., U.K., Germany and several other western countries moved into the region. The American Baptists came to Nagaland and set up their missions in 1867 to work among the Ao Nagas; in 1879 to work among the Lhota Nagas and in 1880 among the Angami Nagas.

The Nagas were exposed to the outside world for the first time during the First World War, when 2000 of them served in France. In 1918, a Naga club was formed. In 1929, they submitted a petition to the Simon Commission, wherein they desired to be left out from the reform scheme for India. The relevant portion reads as follows:

> "Before the British Government conquered our country in 1879-1880, we were living in a state of intermittent warfare with the Assamese of the Assam valley to the North and West of our country and Manipuris in the South. They never conquered us nor were we subjected to their rule. On the other hand, we were always a terror to these people. Our country within the administered area consists of more than eight Tribes, quite different from one another with quite different languages which cannot be understood by each other, and there are more Tribes outside the administered area which are not known at present. We have no Unity among us and it is really the British Government that is holding us together now." (Memorandum of the Naga Hills to Simon Commission on January 10, 1929)

The origins of the word 'naga' or 'nagas' is shrouded in mystery. But its popularization is certainly a nineteenth century phenomenon. For a very long time, the Assamese plains people have called them as 'noga'. The appellation 'nagas' has acquired a generic form that includes more than 30 tribes who live in Nagaland and neighbouring states of Assam, Arunachal Pradesh and Manipur and the bordering nation-state of Myanmar. The tribes of north east India, however, find mention in the Indian epics i.e. the *Ramayana* and the *Mahabharata* as 'kiratas'. And this denotes the entire race of tribes and is more inclusive in nature than another generic term 'Bodos' which denoted a majority of plains tribes since the medieval period. The Ahoms who ruled over Assam and neighbouring hills for over six hundred years (during 1220-1826) have a separate identity of their own as a ruling elite but they married the girls from among the plains tribes as well as caste-Hindus predominantly of the Brahmaputra Valley and are now an Other Backward Classes (OBC).

The Nagas have shared history with the Assamese, Manipuris, Cacharis and the Singphos. There are certain common traits which make it difficult to distinguish the Nagas from other tribes of the north-east. Their languages share certain features even with the distant Munda group of languages of people living in Jharkhand. The institutions like morung and head-hunting have wide currency even outside India. While the Nagas have many similarities/ common traits with the non-Nagas, the intra-Naga differences are at the same time too many. A study of major tribes of Nagaland (Ao, Angami, Sema, Lotha, Rengma, Chakhesang, Yimchunger, Kalya Kongnyu, Konyak, Chang, Sangtam, Phom, Zeme, Liangmei, Rongmei (Zeliangrong), Khiemungan) would reveal that the Nagas differ in their languages, village-polity, social institutions and usages, physical features, temperament, myths of origin and migration, etc. While asserting Naga identity, the similarities between the Nagas and non-Nagas, and intra-Naga differences are often overlooked. Uncritical rejection of facts has led to certain obsessions, bias, subjectivity and myth-making. Such things have happened specially in the case of the Nagas and generally in the north-east.

The Nagas migrated into the Naga Hills from southeast China and Burma over a long period of time. The Naga legends make us believe that all the Naga tribes migrated from Burma across the Somra tracts and reached a place called Khezekenoma just across the border of Manipur. The name Naga was given to them by outsiders. The Nagas resented the name for long, till political expediency caused it to be accepted. The different Naga tribes never lived as one group. Each tribe lived in one village or more but it exclusively belonged to them. Each village was self-sufficient as demands were limited and by and large maintained its independent character. Any interference, trespassing or encroachments by members of other villages (which invariably meant another tribe) in its territorial jurisdiction usually provoked inter village war leading at times to head-hunting.

My description of the Naga society as narrated in my book *The Problem of Change* needs recalling. It reads:

> "The Nagas are not the 'naked' people, as is erroneously understood by the word 'Naga'. Except for the Angami sub-clan, the Nagas are a group who developed strong village institutions under the leadership of a chief and loved their freedom passionately. Stone worship is common among the

Nagas as they believe that they are born of stone. The various tribes of Nagas, each speaking a dialect of its own, had one thing in common and that was their sense of valour. At different periods of history the Nagas have indulged in constant feuds and head-hunting. The Nagas' conflicts with Manipur, the British forces and the security forces in the post-Independence era are well-known. The feud between the Assamese plainsmen bordering Naga territory is almost a constant feature of known history. In their socio-political outlook, while the Nagas accord equal rights to men and women, the women are prevented from participating in politics, fighting and hunting. The political process in Nagaland, in tune with its past traditions, has not sent any significant number of womenfolk to their legislative assemblies. The traditional Naga attitude towards property was one of 'renunciation'. The Feasts of Merit, which bestowed distinction on their donors, was intended to show the virtues of distributing wealth over its possession. While the Feasts of Merit are still in vogue, the attitude towards property has changed. Acquisitiveness is now dominant, and the traditional institution of communal ownership of property is cracking. The process seems irreversible". (pp.30-31)

Language contributes meaningfully to identify formation. The Naga languages belong to the Tibeto Burman family. There are more than eighteen languages spoken by Nagas in Nagaland itself. The prevalence of Nagamese as the language of dialogue among Naga tribes and of the local market is a recent phenomenon and shows predominant influence of Assamese language. The Nagas had a long tradition of visiting the Assam plains and particularly their *weekly hats* (bazars). The rich Christian religious literature put down in Roman script is another feature of Nagaland's linguistic profile. All these reveal great spirit of accommodation in Naga society.

During the Second World War (1939-45), Kohima was a battle ground of the Allied and Axis forces. The journey of the Nagas from a district of Assam to the status of Union Territory and the State has been very quick. The State of Nagaland was inaugurated on 1st December, 1963. The inauguration of Nagaland as a full-fledged state of the Indian Union brought a population of 3.71 lakhs in an area of 16579 sq. kms. at par with the bigger States such as the Uttar Pradesh with 74 million people and 2,94,416 sq. kms area, with the same privileges and status. Nagaland was the first state in the country with such meagre population and small area. It was not formed on linguistic lines nor it conformed to the criteria of economic viability but purely on political consideration. The state was to run and continues to be sustained mainly on the grants received from the Consolidated Fund of India.

The formation of the new state gave birth to never ending demands for small states in the north-east and elsewhere in the country on ethnic lines. Nagaland was replicated in Mizoram. The insurgency in Mizo Hills district of Assam by the Mizo National Front (MNF) under the leadership of Laldenga, and the formation of Mizoram as a State of the Indian Union, was much on the same lines as witnessed in Nagaland. The demands for the formation of Meghalaya by All Party Hill Leaders Conference (APHLC), and similar demands for the full-fledged statehood in Manipur and Tripura got encouragement due to the creation of Nagaland. Thus the statehood of Nagaland was the fore-runner of the reorganization of the north-east. The same may be said about the insurgency in the rest of the region. The Naga insurgency is the mother of all the insurgencies in the north-east India. Fortunately, the re-organisation of north east India got completed by 1972 and successive governments at the Centre have wisely resisted demands for further division of Assam and rationalization of boundaries of States of the region on ethnic lines of exclusivity denying the logic of a plural society.

The Naga identity formation is a recent phenomenon. Many tribes who call themselves Naga today, were unaware of the term. Many Naga tribes were not included into that category even a few decades ago. On the contrary, even Kukis, Cacharis, Abors and many other communities were called Nagas in the nineteenth and early twentieth century. Thus the term 'Naga' was a fluid one. It was a loose term. The Naga identity continues to be an evolving identity. However, politicization of the said identity has led to much myth-making and propaganda. It made the study of the Nagas and their identity necessary in anthropological, cultural and historical perspective to remove the perceptional haziness about the same. The present book is an effort in that direction. Dr. B.B. Kumar sums up his approach as follows:

> "..... the Assamese, who called them 'Noga', the Indian British Government, and to the greatest extent, the Government of Independent India forged and strengthened Naga Unity and thereby their 'greater identity'. Ironically, many Nagas who suffer from 'holier than thou' attitude, blame them the most for keeping them under separate administrative units. The authors long sojourn as an educator in Nagaland and his abiding interest in the history and anthropology of Nagas and other tribal communities of the area was one of the reasons to write this book. The recent movement for greater Nagaland, viz Nagalim, compelled the author to undertake immediate repeat-study of the history and anthropology of the Naga tribes to update and renew the earlier ones. The present book is the outcome of the same. While the recent identity formation and desire of the Nagas to live together, is a welcome development, the same should not be claimed on the basis of history and anthropology; as facts do not substantiate such assertions. At the same time there should not be clash of competing desires to bring complications."

Democracy has greatly contributed to forging of a composite Naga identity in Nagaland. Notwithstanding insurgency and occasional boycott, the forces of insurgency articulated the proud and independent character of the Nagas even as the forces of democracy had used the tradition of democracy in Naga society to make it participate in elections. Fortunately, the democratic forces are having now a upper hand. The small group of people who wanted to secede from India are losing support as democratic processes are gradually integrating the Naga people into the mainstream of economic development and modernization. The nation could reasonably be proud of a moderately stable constitutional culture in Nagaland particularly in the backdrop of the earlier insurgency movements and violence.

The growth of the middle class in Nagaland was intimately linked up with the spread of education and was not based either on a landed aristocracy, which never existed, or on commercial activity, which came only with the introduction of English education. Even here the middle class is the dominant group. It comprises the politicians, bureaucracy, businessmen from contractors to shopkeepers, and those belonging to independent professions, such as law and medicine. The migrant middle class is a product of the massive expenditure on development schemes dating back to the 1960s and consists of contractors, shopkeepers, foodgrain dealers, etc., from North India. They are mainly concentrated in Dimapur, which is outside the purview of 'inner-line'.

The middle class phenomenon in Nagaland has four distinctive features: (1) the absence of a traditional bourgeoisie or capitalist class; (2) the contradictions and conflicts between two easily identifiable groups – the indigenous middle class and the migrant middle class; (3) the control of the indigenous middle class over the apparatus of the State, including the bureaucracy and agriculture, and of the migrant middle class over industry and trade; and (4) the economic leverage commanded by outside business houses.

If 'identity' is to look different, to stand apart from others, the Nagas have a distinct identity in terms of physique, folklores, folktales and world-view. Times have changed them but still they are distinct. And yet at the same time they know interdependence. They have practiced tolerance towards others point of view. They view their future among a community of believers in different faiths and races. Vital fragments of the past still live on in dress, customs, ceremonies, festivals and in their attitudes towards women despite mass conversion to Christianity. The uniqueness of the Nagas lies in their institutions of governance – the villages, the *morungs,* methods and processes of cultivation involving the community, their arts and crafts, their rituals and beliefs; and their lores and tales.

Identity movement should lead to re-creation of memories of tribal life. Unfortunately, not much work is done in this behalf. What is happening is domination of political issues over memories, over stories related to conservation of ecology, over traditional music and dance forms, over common ownership of natural resources.

There are two contradictory forces in operation in Nagaland. One is for democracy, peace and development; and the other for violence, insurgency and extortion. Increasingly the forces of peace are gaining strength and the conclusion of peace with major insurgency groups by the Government of India is bound to herald an era of constructive activity and say of the Nagas not only in their own affairs but in the affairs of the country as a whole.

There should be sincere and imaginative efforts to accord the people of Nagaland powers that could be given to a federating unit that is possible within the constitutional and parliamentary framework of empowerment. The Nagas have a great sense of realism and once it is clear to them that the Government of India is willing to give them all that they could within the framework of the constitution and powers of parliament, it should not be difficult for them to conclude an agreement to end this long period of strife and uncertainty. The empowerment of Naga people and their democratic institutions of governance would lead to peace and amity among the tribes and in its neighbourhood and unprecedented economic and cultural progress.

For a variety of reasons outlined earlier, Nagaland, the sixteenth State of the Indian Union, occupies a significant place in the national consciousness. The end of insurgency in Nagaland and heralding of peace process and launching of massive economic programmes in that State would release the energy of the people in a constructive manner. In the language of a Buddhist monk (infact of a song) **"The snow has fallen, but don't be sad, After the snowfall, comes the warmth of the sun."** The sun is bound to rise not in distant future but in our life-time and illuminate Nagaland and the whole region. The civilisational idea of and democratic realities in India allow regional or local identity to co-exist with national identity without any stress or animosity. A Naga serving in another State or living within Nagaland finds no conflict either of interest or of values in his being a Naga and an Indian simultaneously.

I am sure *Naga Identity* would add to greater understanding that the Naga identity and the Indian identity reinforce each other and support the forces of inclusiveness, dialogue and peace in Nagaland. The book is accordingly commended for wider readership.

26 November, 2004
Guru Nanak Jayanti Day
New Delhi

(Balmiki Prasad Singh)
Chancellor, CIHTS (deemed to be University),
Sarnath and former Union Home Secretary

PREFACE

The Nagas lived in self-sufficient village republics. Most of their villages were located at the hill-tops or on the spurs of the hills. They were well protected against the enemy attack and in many cases, even the sections of the village (*khels*) had their separate defence arrangements. Different clans of a tribe inhabiting a village lived in different quarters (*khels*) of the village. The clan solidarity was the most pronounced phenomenon in the Naga society.

'Naga' is a generic term used for about thirty tribes inhabiting our North-Eastern fringe and across our border in Myanmar. Most of the tribes known as "Naga" today were not aware of the term before the establishment of the Naga Hills district. The Nagas of Tuensang started using the term only after the advent of the administration in that district in the early 1950s and especially after the formation of Naga Hills Tuensang Area. In this case, an interesting encounter with an elderly Chang is worth quoting. He said: "We were calling ourselves Chang. You people came and told us that we are Nagas and we started calling ourselves Nagas. We started learning Hindi, but you told us to learn English. And we started learning English." The Nagas used to call themselves by the respective names of the tribe concerned; but the more pronounced trend was to identify oneself with the village of one's inhabitation. Thus their identity used to be mostly village based.

There is considerable confusion about the Naga identity among the Nagas and the non-Nagas. The Naga identity, as exists today, is a recent construct. It continues to evolve and is a case of greater identity formation. The author attempts in this book to analyze Naga identity formation in the broader framework, taking into consideration their history and culture, origin, migration, ethnicity, social structure and village polity. It also deals with the politicization of the Naga identity. The book aims at removing perceptional haziness about the Naga identity.

Shri B.P. Singh, former Home Secretary, Government of India has kindly written the foreword of the book. The author expresses his grateful thanks for the same. The author is thankful to Shri J.N. Roy, *IPS* (Retd.), treasurer Astha Bharati, for encouragement for writing the book. He also thanks Shri Ashok Kumar Mittal of Concept Publishing Company, New Delhi for speedily undertaking the publication of the book.

B.B. Kumar

CONTENTS

1

INTRODUCTION

The Naga Students Federation (NSF) has issued a directive and a warning against any academic research into the Naga people's history without its permission. The immediate provocation for the directive, as reported, was due to their concern about 'genome research project' which has been undertaken in Nagaland University by some Naga and non-Naga scholars. It requires, among other things, the collection of blood samples from every Naga tribe. The NSF, whose support to Naga nationalist aspirations and Naga sovereignty is well-known, is afraid that such physical anthropological research may reveal, beyond doubt, the physical distinctiveness of different Naga tribes. The NSF maintains that the history of the Naga people had been distorted by the research by non-Naga scholars. The president of the apex Naga students' organization said that 'people from outside the Naga community' would not be allowed to undertake any research on Naga history without the organization's permission (*Frontline,* September 26, 2003). This development makes it clear that the universities; Nagaland University now, and North-Eastern Hill University earlier, have failed to create healthy academic ethos; and the above-mentioned directive is the manifestation of the new form of 'academic terrorism'.

The Britishers kept the Nagas isolated from the rest of the country. Some prominent British colonial functionaries wanted the separation of the Naga and other tribal inhabited areas of the North-East from the rest of the country. Their strategy, commonly known as the Coupland Plan, of the formation of a separate Crown Colony or a Hill State could not succeed as the independence came too early after Second World War for them. The Nagas by and large wanted to remain in India. Their only apex organization, Naga National Council (NNC), passed a resolution just before independence, and wanted the Naga Hills district to remain a part of Assam State in India. The demand of self-determination was made by a section of the Nagas afterwards.

The generic term 'Naga' was loosely used for a number of tribes on our eastern fringe a century ago. Not only the tribes calling themselves Naga today, but even the Kukis, Kacharis, Abors, Mikirs and the Nepalis settled there were called Nagas. On the other hand, even Nagas did not know about the particular nomenclature, and even resented to be called Nagas. Every Naga tribe has its own name. Its neighbours also gave separate name to a tribe. Thus the composite Naga identity is of recent origin and it lacks claimed historical support. The history of the Nagas is the history of the individual tribes; it is also the history of a thousand Naga village republics.

The Nagas had harmonious relationship with the Ahom kings. At least the Aos and the Lothas never raided the plains for the heads. Few cases of the conflict between the Eastern Nagas and the Ahoms is recorded by Gait in his *History of Assam*. But such raids became gradually less and less. Angamis and other Nagas served in the Ahom army. The Naga raids in Assam and Cachar plains started only after the arrival of the Britishers in the North-Eastern scenario. Similar interface existed between the various Naga tribes and Manipuris, Kacharis and Singphos.

The demand of the right of self-determination was voiced by the NNC under the leadership of Phizo. It was based on the grounds of (*i*) ethnic distinctiveness, (*ii*) distinct social life, way of living, laws and customs, etc., and (*iii*) different religion – Animism and Christianity. The Nagas are in noway distinct from other tribes of the region. Their social life, way of living and customs are also dissimilar in many ways. Animism and Christianity are also not the exclusive religions of the Nagas. On one hand, there are many traits, which are not shared by all the Naga tribes, on the other hand, there are many common culture markers, which are shared by the Nagas and the non-Nagas.

The Nagas are polyglot; they speak dozens of mutually un-intelligible languages. The physical features differ even from one household to another in a village. The intra-Naga differences in their social structure, village polity, dress, hair style, tattooing, setting of the village, housing pattern also differ significantly. The mode of agriculture, sowing of seed and harvesting is also not identical. Their mortuary rites and beliefs after death are also not similar. The migration has taken place almost from every direction. But the places of origin are not far away from their present habitat.

The Naga tribes have mixed origin. They have incorporated Mongoloid, Austric, Aryan and even Negroid ethnic elements in them. Even the individual Naga tribes have taken ethnic elements from diverse sources. In spite of such vast diversity, the "greater identity formation" has taken place, which is a welcome development. The Naga identity is a stable one today.

The greater identity formation of the Nagas was only possible by bringing them under single administrative unit of Naga Hills district followed by the unification of Naga Hills and Tuensang area. It became a dense administrative region after the formation of the State. Unprecedented growth of education and development activities brought the Nagas nearer to each other than never before. Even the spread of Christianity was facilitated by the State formation. It was not possible for the Nagas to even know each other without bringing them together under bigger administrative unit. It is interesting to know that even as late as 1929 after the formation of the Naga Hills district the Nagas hardly knew each other. The Memorandum presented to the Simon Commission by the Naga Club gives clear picture of the knowledge of the Nagas about themselves. It says:

> "Our country within the administered area consists of more than eight Tribes, quite different from one another with quite different languages which cannot be understood by each other, and there are more Tribes outside the administered area which are not known at present. We have no Unity among us and it is really the British Government that is holding us together now."

It is clear from the above statement that the Assamese, who called them 'Noga', the Indian British Government, and to the greatest extent, the Government of Independent India forged and strengthened Naga Unity and thereby their 'greater identity'.

Ironically, many Nagas who suffer from 'holier than thou' attitude, blame them the most for keeping them under separate administrative units.

The authors long sojourn as an educator in Nagaland and his abiding interest in the history and anthropology of Nagas and other tribal communities of the area was one of the reasons to write this book. The recent movement for greater Nagaland, *viz.* Nagalim, compelled the author to undertake immediate repeat-study of the history and anthropology of the Naga tribes to update and renew the earlier ones. The present book is the outcome of the same. While the recent identity formation and desire of the Nagas to live together, is a welcome development, the same should not be claimed on the basis of history and anthropology; as facts do not substantiate such assertions.

2

THE NAGAS : AN OVERVIEW

Naga is a generic term used for about thirty tribes of our eastern hill frontier in the states of Nagaland, Manipur, Arunachal Pradesh and Assam. The Angami, Ao, Chakhesang, Chang, Khiamnungan, Konyak, Lotha, Phom, Pochury, Rengma, Sangtam, Sema, Yimchungru and Zeliang reside in the state of Nagaland. Chakhesang, known earlier as Eastern Angami, is the combination of Chokri, Kheja and Sangtam (better known as Pochury) tribes. Zeliang is the combination of Zemi and Liangmei. Similarly, Zeliangroung is the combination of Zemi, Liangmei and Roungmei tribes. The Tangkhul, Mao, Maram, Kabui (also known as Roungmei), Kachcha (Zemi), Koireng (Liangmei), Maram, Maring, Thangal, Anal, Moyon, Monsang and Lamgang Nagas reside in northern, north-western and eastern districts of Manipur. It needs mention that the Anals were earlier considered to be a Kuki-Chin tribe and they speak a language of that family; but they claim now to be a Naga tribe. Rengma and Zemi Nagas also reside in Karbi Anglong and North Cachar Hills districts of Assam, Noctes, Wanchos and Tangsas live in Tirap and Changlang districts of Arunachal Pradesh. Some Naga tribes also reside in Myanmar in the contiguous areas of Tirap, Mon, Tuensang and East Manipur, especially in the Somra tract. They are Heimei, Para, Rangpan, Htangan, Tsaplaw and Somra Nagas.[1] Khiamnungan, Tikhir, Chirr and Makaware tribes found in Tuensang district are also living across the border.[2] Khiamnungans are called Para in Myanmar.

Origin of the Word "Naga"

The nomenclature 'Naga' was given to these people by the Assamese. They pronounce it *'Noga'*. The opinion about the origin of the word 'Naga' differs. Capt. Butler linked the term with Hindi word *'nanga'* and Bengali word *'nangta'*, and some with Sanskrit *'nagna'*. These words mean naked. Gait, Peal, Holecombe and Elwin link it with the word 'nok' (meaning people in Nocte; Sanskrit *'loka'*, people). Owen favours the derivation of the term from Sanskrit, *'nag'*, meaning mountain.[3]

Hutton favours its derivation from the Sanskrit *'nagna'*. He wrote:

> "In view of the fact that Ptolemy in the third or the fourth century A.D. and Shiabuddin Talish in the sixteenth both speak of Nagas as "Nanga," *qua* "naked," I must recant my derivation of "Naga" from the Sanskrit Nag (*vide* Mills, The *Lhota Nagas*, p. xvi, n.2) and substitute the Sanskrit *nagna*. See Yule and Burnell, Hobson Jobson (1903), S. V. NAGA. The correspondent who would derive "naga" from *Nok* (Hindustani log?) was probably S.E. Peal, and was certainly in error."[4]

E.T. Dalton has also linked the term 'Naga' to the Sanskrit root, meaning 'naked' or the Sanskrit *'Nag'*, snake. He wrote:

> "The learned leave us to take our choice as to whether the term Naga, the name applied by the Hindus to the inhabitants of the hills we are about to explore, is from the Sanskrit root, meaning 'naked', or the Sanskrit *'Nag'*, snake. Whichever derivation we take, it must be admitted that the word is aptly applied, as the Nagas love to decorate, rather than to clothe, their person, and are decidedly snake-like in their habits."[5]

The Austric link with *Nag* (snake) legend is well established. Some Naga languages certainly show marked Munda, an Austric language, linguistic traits. Therefore, the possibility of derivation of the word from *'Nag'* should be examined.[6]

The Use of the Term "Naga"

As mentioned earlier the name "Naga" to these tribes was given by others. Until recently, the term was not in general use among the Naga people.[7] The people of Tuensang rarely spoke of themselves as Naga even in 1954.[8] The same was the case with the Nagas of Cachar. Soppit observes: "Many of the people from intercourse with the plains began to acknowledge the term Nage and to answer to it, but in the remoter villages, removed from outside influence, the term is unknown, nor is it in anyway recognised by surrounding tribes, Kukis and Kacharis".[9] Not only this term was not used by the Nagas themselves, but in fact, as Hokishe Sema has observed, "for long, this appellation of "Naga" was resented to by these people, till political expediency caused it to be accepted as describing the separate identity of these people as distinct from other ethnic tribal people and also from the people in the country at large.[10]

Earlier, the term 'Naga' was loosely used for other tribes also. As for example, we find mention of the "Kachari Nagas", "Kuki Nagas" and the "Abor Nagas" in the nineteenth century by Dalton.[11] Hutton's observation about the Nagas in this connection is worth quoting, which says: "if not impossible, it is exceedingly difficult to propound any test by which a Naga tribe can be distinguished from other Assam or Burma tribes which are not Nagas."[12] On the other hand, there exists too much intra-Naga differences. Anyway, the Naga identity formation, though new, and to large extent artificial construct was a welcome development. B.K. Roy Burman has termed it "Secondary Social Entity.[13] It is a case of "Greater Identity Formation."[14]

The Names of the Individual Tribes

Most of the Naga tribes use different names for themselves than the names commonly given to them. In most of the cases, even their neighbours also call them differently. The names of some of the Naga tribes is given below:

Commonly used Name of the Tribe	*Other Name*(s)
Ao	They call themselves Ao and Aorr; called Ao by Chang Nagas; Aorr by Sangtams; Cholimi by Semas; Uri or Chongli by Lothas, Paimi by Konyaks, Hatigoria and Dupdoria by the Assamese.
Angami	Call themselves Tengima and Tenyimie. Earlier they were called Gnamei and Tsanglo. They are called Monr by Ao Tsungumi by Semas and Tsungung by Lothas.

Commonly used Name of the Tribe	*Other Name*(s)
Sema	Called Sema by Angamis; Simi, Simrr by Chongli Aos; Moiyarr by Mongsen Aos; Chumm by Lothas; Sumrr by Sangtams; Samgli by Changs.
Lotha	Ndreng or Southern Lothas call themselves Kyong, "Kyon or Okyo; called Chisima by Angamis; Tsindrr by Aos and Choimi by Sema, Miklei by Assamese and Tsontsu by themselves.
Rengma	They called themselves Njong or Injang; called Monr by Aos, Mozhumi by Angamis, Moiyui by Lothas, Mezama by Angamis and Moxhumi by Semas.
Konyak	People of Tamlu called themselves Konyak or Haha; called Mirirr by Aos; Taprongami or Minyuma Nagamni by Semas; and by various names like Banpara, Mutonia, Namsangia, Tablungia etc. by the Assamese.
Chang	They are called Mojung by Konyak, Mochungrr by Aos; Mochunmi by Semas, and Machongrr by Sangtams.
Phom	Also known in odd days as Tamlu and Chingmengnu Nagas; Phoms of Mirenokpo or Assiringia villages in Ao area were called Assiringia Nagas by the Assamese.
Sangtam	Called themselves Isachnure or Bir Pirr; called Lophomi (Northern Sangtam) and Tukomi (Central Sangtam) by Semas, Sangtam by Changs and Sangtamrr by Aos. Eastern Sangtam together with Chokri and Kheja is called Chakhesang and alone Pochuri.
Yimchunger	The tribe called itself Yachongr. Called Yachumi by Sems, Yamsongrr by Aos; Yamsung by Changs and Yamchongrr by Sangtams.
Khiamngan	Called themselves Khiamngan (alternative spelling Khemungam, Khemungan, Khiemungan); called Aoshed by Changs; Tukhemni by Semas and Para in Burma. Early name also Kolyokengnyu (the one living in stone roofed houses); also known as Bosorr.

Commonly used Name of the Tribe	*Other Name*(s)
Kheja	Known as Chakhesang along with Chokri and Sangtam (Eastern); also known as Kezhama, Kezami and Eastern Angami.
Chokri	Also known as Chakhesang; Eastern Angami, Chakru and Chakrima.
Zemi	Known as Zeliang with Liangmei and Zeliangrong with Liangmei and Rongmei Nagas; called Mezame by Angamis; other name is Kachcha Nagas.
Liangmei	Old name is Koireng.
Rongmei	(Nruanghmei) are also known as Kabui or Kachcha Nagas.
Mao	Called themselves Memi.

Classification of the Naga Tribes

The Naga tribes were roughly classified into the following four categories:

The Southern Nagas

This included Zemi, Liangmei, Ruongmei, and some Naga tribes of Manipur. The classification is based on linguistic differences, advanced mode of singing and dancing among Zeliangrong Nagas, prevalence of Technonimy among the Zemi and the existence of Morung as an important institution and feature of the village.

Western Nagas

The Western Nagas include Angamis, Chakhesangs, Semas, Rengmas, Lothas, Maos and Marams. They share the legend of dispersal of the tribes from Kezekenoma stone, practise stone pulling ceremony (except the Semas), bury their dead and cover the paddy seeds after dispersal with earth by using Hoe. Angamis practise extensive terraced cultivation. These Nagas do not practise tattooing. Heads taken during head-hunting were burnt or hung outside the village.

Central Nagas

This category includes Aos, Tangkhuls, Sangtams, Changs, Phoms, Yimchungrus and Khiamngans. They practised tattooing, used to make xylophones (large wooden war drums), out of single tree trunk and used to hang the head taken in war in their houses. They do not cover the paddy seed after dispersal and do not practise stone pulling ceremony. These Nagas used to expose their dead on machans; some also smoked the dead body. The Chang also used to bury their dead. The Sangtams buried the dead body below hearth throwing out any bone found during digging.The Tangkhuls used to bury the dead and erected machan over the grave, as the Aos did.

Eastern Nagas

The Eastern Nagas include the Konyaks, Wanchos, etc. They practised exposure of the dead, but used to treat the head separately. Tattooing was extensively practised. They made huge war drum from single tree trunk.

Physical Features/Characteristics

The Nagas tribes differ considerably in their physical features, appearance, general characteristics; dress, ornaments, weapons, cultural and social set up, languages, etc. Such differences are found from place to place and even within a single tribe. In many cases, it is not possible to give any general description of the features of even a single tribe. As Hutton has observed in the case of the Angami Nagas: "it would be impossible to give any general description of the type of Angami features, as it varies from village to village and even from house to house in a remarkable degree. The flattened nose and slightly oblique eyes of a decidedly Mongolian type may be seen side by side with a straightness of eyes and nose that might be purely Aryan."[15] In spite of such wide-ranging differences the contrasting features of different tribes have been observed and reported by many scholars. It may be interesting to describe some of them.

Dr. Brown gave common name 'Kolya' Nagas to a collectivity of Naga tribes consisting of eight clans, namely, Thangal, Mao, Murram, Pural, Threngba, Meithiphum, Myang-Khong, and

Tokpo-Khul (in reality, the first three are known tribes; the identity of the rest is not known). The Kolyas occupy geographically intermediate position. They may be said to resemble the Kaupuis[16] in the south, to blend into the Angamis on the north, to approximate to the Tankhuls to the east, and to gradually become more and more like the Kachcha Nagas on the north and north-west isolated, however, within their respective wild mountain homes the various clans of Kolyas have come to possess peculiarities in dress, social habits, and language which render it no difficult task to assign to each man his proper clan, if not to fix the very village to which he belongs. They have little or no dealings with each other, but on the contrary exist in what one might be almost pardoned for describing as a chronic and hereditary state of feud one with the other.....Their custom differ but slightly from those of the Kaupuis, but in language, dress, and facial peculiarities they are much more nearly related to the Angamis."[17] This shows intra-tribal differences in language, dress, customs, etc. among the Nagas.

The Angami Naga, with considerable physical powers and great power of endurance is ordinarily about five feet nine inches tall. The stature, tall for a hillsman, not infrequently goes upto six feet. The men of Khonoma group are generally made on rather heavier lines and are on a whole taller than the Chakhesangs.[18] The body of the Angami, as Hutton observes, "is lithe and frequently very finely developed, particularly to the calf and chest and shoulders, for which the climbing of hills and hoeing of terraced fields are doubtless responsible.[19] The toes of the Angamis are often widely separate, the big toe branching away from the others. Angami's features are mobile, pleasant and often decidedly handsome, and the voice on the whole musical.[20] John Butler in his *'Rough Notes on the Angami Nagas'* has written about their physique and characteristics. He wrote: "The average Angami is a fine, hardy, athletic fellow, brave and war-like, and among themselves, as a rule, most truthful and honest. On the other hand, he is blood-thirsty, treacherous, and revengeful to an almost incredible degree. This, however, can scarcely be wondered at when we recall what I have already related regarding revenge being considered a most holy act, which they have been taught from childhood ever to revere as one of their most sacred duties.[21]

The Ao men, as observed by A.W. Davis, in *Census of India, 1891,* Assam (Vol. 1), both Chongli and Mongsen, are somewhat darker in complexion and inferior in physique to the Angamis. The women, who are comparatively superior in physique to the men, are, after the Angamis, the best looking in the hills.[22] The Sema men are short and muscular.[23] Lothas inhabit, comparatively warmer area which has its effect on their physique. The tribe was adjudged to be most quiet and amenable to discipline.[24] In a comparison, it is said that 'if the Sema among Naga tribes be likened to the Irishman then the Lotha is the Scot among them.'[25] The Rengmas and the Kacharis are found to be similar.[26] The Kachcha Nagas compare unfavourably in physique with the Angamis; being less muscular built but well made and active. The tribe is simple and honest in character, with a ready appreciation of honour.They compare favourably with Kacharis and Kukis in appearance, having often well-cut features, and bright, intelligent faces. The flat noses and high cheekbones are not uncommon. They are not a war-like tribe.[27] Tangkhuls and Luhupas are a tall race.[28] Marings resemble Burmans.[29] The physique of the northern tribes is considered to be inferior and black.[30]

The Chang Nagas, having fine tall but lean physique, are very war-like tribe. Hutton observes: "The tribe is very war-like, being second to none, not excepting the Semas. They are of fine physique, tall but lean."[31] He further observes, "The Chang has stature, but not the breadth, not the calf, being rather curiously built on very marked lines of his own tall, lean and narrow, though muscular enough."[32] They usually have red or light brown skin and wavy hair. The black complexion is looked down with contempt and aversion and white as decidedly unpleasing. The Nagas with red skin as attribute are called "matmei" or real men.[33] The observation of Porteus about them is worth quoting:

> "I should say, their physique is good for Nagas and superior to that of Aos and Lothas,. ...they seem not to be wanting in pluck as estimated by the Naga standard....I should be inclined to differ from Macabe's opinion....that they have any affinity to the Semas. The connection between them and the Aos seems on the contrary, to be a near one as might be expected from their geographical position.... Although absolutely cut off

from all communication with the plains, I should place the Majungs[34] decidedly higher in the scale of civilization than the Semas, and hardly below the Aos.[35]

The Lotha's colour varies from light to medium brown. The inhabitants of the low ranges tends to be darker.[36]

Dresses and Ornaments

The Nagas differ in their dress and ornaments, pattern of cloths, especially in the patterns of their beautiful shawls. Dr. Butler has written: "I may here note that, like our own Scotch Highlanders, every Naga tribe uses a peculiar pattern of cloth, and thus any individual can at once be easily identified by his tartan."[37]

Colonel R.G. Woothorpe has divided the Nagas of the Naga Hills and the country to the north of the Angamis into kilted and non-kilted Nagas. The Kabuis and many of the Kolyas used to wear a figleaf-like apron suspended from the waist string, or to don a sort of tightly bound *dhoti* which covered their back as well as the front of the body. The *dhoti* worn by the Mao and Murram Kolyas, however, very much resembled the Angami Naga black kilt, only that the ornamental shells on it never (as formerly was the case amongst the Angamis) denoted a warrior who had captured so many human heads. The Kolyas as a race are, however, far inferior to the Angamis or even to the Kabuis in matters of personal adornment. The Mao and Murram Nagas rarely wore any other garment besides their black kilt, and only occasionally did they possess ornaments or jewelleries. Their ears were, however, perforated by persons who desired to wear earrings during the winter months, and coloured cotton thread, red and blue, was worked into ear pendants eight inches long.[38]

The chief article of attire of the Angamis, and one which distinguishes him from most other Nagas, used to be, and still is, during special occasions, a kilt of blue or black cotton cloth of home manufacture, varying from 3 ½ to 4 ½ feet in length, according to the size of the man, and about 18 inches in width, decorated with three, and sometimes, though very rarely, with four, horizontal rows of small white cowrie-shells. This kilt, as stated by John Butler, "passes round the hips and overlaps in front, the edge of the upper flap is ornamented with a narrow fringe, whilst the under-flap having a string attached to its lower corner is pulled up tightly between the legs, and the string, which generally has a small courie attached to the end of it, is then either allowed to hang loosely a few inches below the waist belt, or is tucked in at the side, and thus the most perfect decency is maintained, forming a pleasing contrast to some of their neighbours 'who walk the tangled jungle in mankind's primeval pride'."[39]

He further remarks about the Angami dress: "I do not think that any dress that I have ever seen, tends so much to show off to the very best advantage all the points of a really fine man, or so ruthlessly to express all the weak points of a more weedy specimen as this simple courie begirt kilt."[40] And again he praises that dress eloquently thus: "Finally, as regards the dress of the Angami, I do not think that we can easily find a more picturesque costume anywhere than that of the men, but it requires to be seen to be understood, and I am afraid no amount of description can adequately represent the vivid colours, and general get-up of a well-dressed Angami warrior, flashing about in all his gala war-paint,..."[41]

Aos in the earlier days were known as Hattigorias, Dupdorias. The Phom Nagas of Mirinokpo, a colony from Orangkong, were known as Assiringias. R.G. Woodthorpe has described their dress as given below:

> "Dress of the three tribes is the same, consisting for the males of a small waist-cloth tied at the back end, being brought round between the legs and drawn up under the waist-belt, falls in front in a broad flap. These cloths are of various colours and patterns, from dark blue with white stripes, to white with variegated patterns of black, or black and crimson. The Dupdorias fix small stripes of brass in clusters down the edges of their flaps, apparently to give them additional weight. The broad dark blue or black flap adorned with cowries is also common among these tribes in full dress. The general decorations ...as being worn by the non-kilted tribes, such as the bearskin corone, cotton wool bindings for the hair, and puffs for the ears, necklaces, etc. There is one common ornament worn suspended on the chest,...it is a long flat strip of wood about 15 inches long, narrow in middle, but

broadening slightly towards the ends, and covered with coloured canework, cowries or white seeds, and adorned with a fringe of long red-hair....The Assiringias wear in war dress, tall conical helmets, adorned with boar's tusks and two straight plumes of hair, one on each side, leaving the apex of the helmet bare. The clothes of these three tribes are many coloured, and seem to be used indiscriminately, according to the taste of the wearer...The women's dress consists of a small petticoat of dark blue, a cloth of the same colour being thrown over the shoulders. They wear large brass rings on each brow, supported by a string passing round the head. Sometimes these rings pass through the upper portion of the ear, but generally they simply hang on the temples. The lobe of the ear supports large thick, oval, or oblong-shaped pieces of a crystal obtained from the plains.[42]

Colonel Woodthorpe describes tail used by the Rengmas, the nakedness of some tribes and the war dress of some of them. According to him: "The Rengma's are particularly noticeable for the peculiar tail which they alone, I believe, of all the tribes wear. It is of wood, about a foot and half long curved upwards, broad at the base and tapering to the tip. Rows of white seeds are fastened longitudinally on the tail, and from it hang long tufts of black, and scarlet hair. The broad part of the tail is fitted to the small of the back, and is suspended from the shoulders by a broad prettily embroidered belt (white, red and black); a small cloth tied tightly round the waist further secures the tail. The tail is used in fight to signify defiance;..." "This tribe, as also many others, wears, as a waist cloth only, a small flap of cotton cloth pendant from the waist belt. Others wear a double flap, the inner end of which is drawn tightly up between the legs and secured at the back to the waist belt. Some of these flaps are dark blue ornamented with cowries, in stars or stripes, others are white with broad red patches, or white with fine red lines: indeed this small garment varies in size, colour, and ornamentation with every village, certainly with every tribe. Some tribes go perfectly naked; One tribe we found close to the Sehmahs, and it is curious fact that these naked people are not found in a group by themselves, but scattered about among the other tribes; thus we find a village of naked Nagas surrounded by decently clad people, and pass through several villages before coming again upon the naked folk. It is very seldom indeed that any women are seen in a state of complete nudity, and generally they are decently clad, much as the Angami women already described. Some tribes, as Rengmas, Lhotas, Hatigorias, etc., supplement their waist cloths by an apron about a foot square, profusely ornamented with cowries; other tribes those in the hills adjoining the districts of Sibsagar and Jaipur, wear a long bright blue cloth, very much embroidered with red cotton, and decorated with beads, the inevitable cowries, etc. Very few, however, of the non-kilted tribes quite come up to the Angami in general appearance, when fully equipped in his war paint: no decorations, though frequently more elaborate, seem so clean or handsome."[43]

The traditional dress of the Lothas is slightly more decent (than Rengma's) and consists, for the men of a small loin-cloth and apron either of light blue or white striped horizontally with thin lines of red, or, for the lower villages, of dark blue striped with broad lines of red. They used to wear a cloth of alternate broad stripes of white and dark blue round the shoulders and reaches to the knee.... The women used to wear a scanty black petticoat and leave the breasts bare. Their ornaments are brass and white metal armlets, beads, and ear ornaments made of small bamboo tubes, into the end of which are inserted small tufts of red hair.[44] A.W. Davis, in Census of India, (1891, Assam, Vol. I) has described Sema dress thus: "They are practically naked, as the small flap they wear dangling from their waists cannot be said to in any way hide their nakedness. In addition to this flap they wear the large cloth common to all the Naga tribes. The commonest pattern among them is a cloth with alternate broad stripes of white and dark blue. The ornaments of the men are beads. In their ears they often wear enormous quantities of cotton.... Their women wear a very scanty black petticoat, and leave their breasts bare. For ornaments they wear strings of beads round their waists and necks, and on their arms brass bracelets. Above their elbow, large and very heavy armlets made of some white metal are usually worn."[45]

The traditional dress of the Changs, like that of Yimchungru and Sangtam, and the Sema *lapuchoh* is a small *lengta* worked in red dog's hair and with a circle of cowries.[46] The Chang shawls are very handsomely designed. Unmarried boys and girls wear the shawls called *Kaksi nei*. Newly married couple use *silang nei.* Yet another veriety of shawl, *tobu nei* has zigzag pattern in alternate red and black on a blue band.[47] Changs, like Semas and Konyaks, used fibre-cloths earlier and there was a time when even fibre cloth was not available in their society. Hutton has written:

> "Fibre-cloth undoubtedly preceded cotton-cloth and among the Changs too there are villages where cotton cloths are not known, while those that have taken to cotton are aschewing fibre. They have a tradition that a few generations ago even fibre-cloths were unknown, and women wearing plantain leaves for the petticoats carried their children in net-bags on their backs, having no other cloths for their children. This tradition, no doubt, indicates the development of cloth from nets. The fibre used by Changs for both nets and fibre-cloth is that of nettle, called by them *seno.*[48]

The Changs use very noticeable belt, which is four to six inches broad band usually completely covered with cowries and sometimes with circles of the same and decorated with red dog's hair.[49] It needs mention that the dog's hair, the circle made of the cowries, etc. have different symbolic meanings. As Hutton observes: "The red dog's hair, like the red goat's hair on dao-handle and sash, is explained as representing the fire, which they apply to the enemy's village; the cowri circle represents the moon, and the trefoil and quatrefoil groups of three or four cowries each, with which they embroider 'lengtas' and belts represents the stars, as raids are undertaken by nights by the light of the moon and the stars".[50] It is believed that the broad cowri belts and cane leggings of the Chang are the survival of the rawhide armour used long ago by them and few other tribes.[51]

The Changs, like Rengmas, used to wear full dress warrior's apron. The use of the Chang warrior's apron and the brass-disc, which is even now used by ex-head-hunters during ceremonial war dances, was denied to anybody who was not a head-hunter.[52] The Changs once extensively used close fitting type cane leggings manufactured by the Khiamngans.[53] Such leggings, still used during ceremonial occasions, were traded to the Aos by them.[54] The Changs wear the hat made of bear's skin ornamented with pairs of small boar's tushes. They purchased from the Khiamngans, a kind of tall conical hat, of fine red plaited cane with a pattern in yellow orchid stalk worked into it, and traded it to the Aos.[55] The decorated ceremonial warrior's helmets with hornbill feathers. Chang ornaments, like those of the Phoms, included large, smooth ivory armlet about two inches broad, consisting of section cut from a tusk. Aos, Angamis, Semas and Lothas also use such armlets with slight variation.[56]

The Changs are good wood carvers, cane workers and excellent poker work decorators. They decorate drinking horn pipes, dao slings and other wood work by their poker work. The axe-shaped dao used by the eastern Rengmas,[57] and the Lothas and themselves a few generations ago,[58] was made by them. The Lothas called it Tsonak. They manufactured beautiful red hafts of spears and traded the same to the Aos, and through the Aos to the northern Rengmas.[59]

The Tangkhul dress consisted of a simple cloth worn round the waist. They tie it in a knot in front leaving the ends hanging down. Their waist cloths are made of stout cotton woven in red and blue stripes two inches wide and horizontal. In cold weather, they wear a long cloth in red and blue stripes over the body. In the case of the chiefs, as per the custom, a handsome border is added to the same. They have another pattern of the dress also. At a time they have a ring on and even if scantily dressed, they consider themselves to be properly garbed. They use much more elaborate costumes on high days and holidays, which consists of a handsome kilt embroidered with ornaments like sequins and the head dress is the luhup with decorations of toucan feathers and tresses of hair. The women wear petticoats, reaching from the waist to the knee, made of the cotton cloth manufactured in the weaving villages with red and white or black and white, two inches in width. Occasionally the women with some pretence to wealth or position wear petticoats of red with small stripes of white and black.[60]

The ordinary dress of the Mao, Maram and Mayang Khong Nagas consists of a short black cotton kilt about eighteen inches deep and ornamented by three or four rows of white cowries. White trouser buttons also, on latter days, replaced the cowries. The rows of cowries were only allowed in the kilts of the persons killing two persons. The use of 'tail' as a curious ornament reminds us of the tail used by the Rengmas. The headman and the persons who have erected a stone wear special cloths. The fashion of the enterprising Angamis also spread among them as they received many clothes from them by barter. The dress of the Kabuis used to be scanty. In the Manipur valley and in Cachar they adopted either a kilt or a short *dhoti* put on Bengali fashion.The Quoirengs/Liangmeis wear the short black kilt, which is the dress of their Angami neighbours with whom they had trade relations.[61] Hodson has quoted the interesting account of the dresses of the Marrings given by Dr. Brown.

> "Their dress consists, amongst both men and women, of a sheet, white with a striped border, or striped throughout; this is folded across the waist and twisted or tucked in at the side; the men fasten one end behind, dhoti-wise; in the women this is allowed to hang down, so as to form a petticoat."[62]

Hodson further notes the similarity between kilt and *dhoti.* He writes:

> "It is noteworthy that the development of the simplest clothing found among these tribes, the plain waist-cloth with fringed ends, leads to both the kilt and the *dhoti,* for both these garments are fastened below in much the same way and differ only in depth."[63]

The upper garment of the Maring men is a sheet of thick cotton, either striped or checked, and sometimes a woollen blanket. The women use a white sheet with striped borders, worn like the Manipuri farak (fanek) and reaching from over the bust to a little way below the knee as the upper garment. The women also wear a sheet like the men's. They also use Manipuri 'furit' or jacket during the cold weather.[64]

The traditional upper garment in India was always an unstitched sheet of cloth or shawl. The material used for the same—whether cotton, wool or silk—depended on local availability and the demands of weather. The thickness of the shawl also depended on the weather condition. The design and the pattern varied from place to place and people to people.

The dress also effects the general appearance of the people. In many cases, it becomes difficult to distinguish the persons of different communities if they put on the same dress.[65]

The dresses and ornaments invariably show social distinction in any society. This is true in the case of the Nagas also. The pattern of the shawls differ indicating prowess in war, feasts of merit and performance of social gennas. Among all the Nagas, only the warriors, who have taken a head, have the right to wear the tail feathers of the great hornbill, and those who have not done so are allowed to wear merely some substitute, or else imitation feathers made of paper.[66]

Hair-dressing

Different kinds of hair-dressing is in vogue among the Naga tribes. The Angamis used to let the hair grow naturally in front while tying up a small knot at the back. The hair going to form the knot was separated from the rest by a narrow circle of shaved skin. This was, however, omitted by the Chakhesangs. The Khejas, in certain cases, allowed the back hair to fall untied to the neck. The Aos, Semas, Lothas, Rengmas, Sangtams, Changs and Yimchungrus used to shave the lower hair and allowed the hair at the top of their head to grow long, cutting it off to the same length all round the head. The Kachcha Naga did not seem to do his hair at all. The Konyaks used to grow a long tail at the back. It reached sometimes to the ground, which instead of being plaited, was tied round with a cloth into an elaborate knot. The Tangkhuls used to cut their hair back at the sides, leaving a point in front. It gave a short of cockscomb effect. A dao and some sort of wooden hammer was employed for that primitive method of hair cutting, in which the dao was held under the hair and tapped along the edge with wooden hammer.[67] The Nagas of Manipur have also their different styles of hair-dressing.[68] In many tribes young girls were only allowed to grow hair after attaining the age of marriage. The stone-puller is not allowed to shave his hair for 30 days.[69]

Tattooing

Tattooing may be considered as some sort of personal decoration. It is practised by all the northern and eastern Nagas, and not by the western Nagas.[70] Among the Konyaks, only the Thendu section tattoos their faces. The Thenkoh section do not do so. The men are married after taking a head. The women of the two sections have different tattoo patterns.[71] Only the women were tattooed among the Aos. They were tattooed on the chin, neck, bosom, arms, and leg. The tattoo pattern for the Chongli and Mongsen women on the legs and arms differed.[72] Only women were tattooed among Sangtams also.[73] Both men and women among the Phoms were tattooed.[74] Among the Changs the head-takers were tattooed on the chest, the women were tattooed on their forehead and chin.[75]

Weapons

The spear, dao and shield are the traditionally used weapons of most of the Naga tribes. The shields used by the Angamis in war used to be a long strip of rhinoceros, elephant or buffalo hide from 5 to 7 feet high, but generally about 5 or 5 ½ feet. A lighter shield made of bamboo was used for ceremonial purposes.[76] Among the other tribes the shields are smaller and less decorated than the Angami's, and among the tribes immediately adjoining the Angamis they are made of plaited bamboo, unadorned generally.... The spears and daos among the Rengmas, Semas, etc., are very similar in appearance and size to those of the Angamis, some slight peculiarity in the shape of the spear occasionally indicating the tribe using it. We find among these non-kilted tribes very good bows and cross-bows of bamboo, carrying long iron-headed arrows, which are seldom poisoned.[77] Lotha's arms are spear, dao and shield[78] Sema's arms are spear, cross-bow and dao.[79] The Chakhesang's two handled dao with a somewhat shorter blade, with the same breadth throughout, had indented end. The Angamis, unlike the Semas, Aos and Changs, have neither their daos decorated with red hair, nor the wooden sling used by them is ornamented to any appreciable extent. The Lotha, Sema and Ao slings almost always have a pattern cut into them. The double bladed dao used by the Chakhesang Nagas, a most uncommon one, was perhaps imported from the Tangkhuls.[80] Daos used by the Changs has a very long blade and long handles and is drawn over the right shoulder.[81] The Changs were expert in the use of cross-bow. The tribes of Tuensang, like the Changs and Khiamngans used to apply poison in the cross-bows.[82]

Naga Village

The attitude of the Nagas towards their villages differ considerably. Some tribes have deep attachment for their village sites and rarely change it, while some of them change it easily. Zemi Nagas, even if they rarely change their village site due to very pressing reason, hardly move a mile away from the old site. This leads one to conjecture that they are descendants of the earlier settlers of the region.[83]

We have very big Ao and Angami villages, whereas the Sema villages are usually small. The Sema villages, like other Naga villages, are situated on the tops of ridges or hills. They are practically without artificial defences of any kind. Semas, like most other Naga tribes, except in the case of a few villages, which have copied the Angami custom, keep, their grain in small granaries clear of the houses of the village. It is, therefore, safe in the case of fire.[84]

Whereas most of the Naga villages are situated on the hill tops or spus, the Tangkhul and Kabui villages are also located on the slopes of the hills. The Tangkhul villages are big and small.[85] Some non-Naga tribes, such as Sauria Pahariyas of Chhota Nagpur also prefer hill-tops for their village sites.[86]

The Naga villages are usually divided into *khels* or sections. Earlier, only one clan lived in a particular *khel.* In many cases even *khels* were well-protected and fortified, as was the case of the Chang Naga villages.[87] The Angami and Ao Nagas had very big villages. Of course, some of their villages were also small. The Naga villages were well-protected also. The following description of the Angami villages makes the picture clear:

> "The Angami villages are invariably built on the very summits of the hills, and vary much in size, some containing as many as a thousand houses, while others consist of no more than twenty. The villages are all strongly fortified with stockades, deep ditches, and massive stone walls, and the hill-sides thickly studded with *panjis*, a *chevaux de fries* of sharp pointed bamboo sticks planted in the ground. In some cases, also, the sloping side of the hill is cut away so as to form a perpendicular wall. The approaches to the villages are tortuous, narrow, covered ways, only wide enough to admit the passage of one man at a time; these lead to gates closed by strong, heavy wooden doors, with look-outs on which a sentry is posted day and night when the clans are at feud. Very often these

approaches are steeply scarped, and only means of entry in the village is by means of a ladder consisting of a single pole, some fifteen or twenty feet high, cut into steps."[88]

A peculiarity in all the villages of the non-kilted Naga tribes, which again distinguishes them from the Angami, is the presence in their villages of a conspicuous building called Bachelor's House or morung. It is also found among the Garos and many other tribes. In larger villages we find two or three of these houses in each village. In these live all the young men of the village, from the age of puberty till such time as they marry and set up a house for themselves. Among the Rengmas, Lothas, etc., the bachelor's house is not a very imposing-looking building, being only rather longer than the other houses in the village, all of which are small and poor as compared with those of most other tribes.[89]

The founding of a Naga village preceded selection of the site and certain rituals. The availability of ample fertile agricultural land and water sources and defence aspect were taken into consideration. The founder, and latter on his descendants, used to be the chief. The first step towards the establishment of a village was to build a morung. All the villagers participated in the construction of the same. The construction of the houses of the priest and the founder followed. It was not possible to settle a village with only one or two clans. An easily defensible place and a tree suitable to be the head-tree was necessary for selecting a site for founding the village by the Rengmas.[90] The water used to be stolen from the parent village by them.[91] The founder and the first settlers usually got better and more land. Latter ones got less and inferior land.[92] The post of the Lotha chief (*ekyung*) was hereditary in the family of the founder of the village.[93] In the case of the Angamis, it was the post of the priest (*kemovo*). Availability of water and a suitable head-tree was necessary for selection of site by the Lothas.[94] The Lotha settlers steal a branch of the head-tree (*mingetung*),[95] water from the village spring[96] and if possible the luck-stone from the parent village.[97] They select a priest (*puthi*).[98] The founder makes fire from the fire-stick.[99]

The villages were, usually, settled on long narrow spurs having a narrow street in between. Many bigger villages in the Angami area, such as Kohima, did not follow such pattern. Tuensang, more than hundred years ago, called Mojung-Jami at that time, was a long narrow village covering about one and a half miles. It looked like a single street with rows of houses on either side.[100]

Housing

Mostly, the traditional Naga houses are either of machan type or those constructed on level ground. A common practice, though, not adopted by the Angami, is that of raising the house above the ground on poles or piles of bamboo. The house is divided generally into a front room, the floor of which is the ground itself, and here is the fireplace. Then we come to a house occupying the rest of the house, the floor of which is raised, and beyond the house is a small raised platform, a continuation of the floor, on which many of the household duties are performed, and where vegetables are dried, etc. The walls and floor of the house are of bamboo matting, with thatched roofs. Not only the northern tribes, but even some Zeliangroung houses are machan or platform structures. The Angamis, Semas, Rengmas, Tangkhuls and the tribes south of them build their houses on ground. The Aos and the northern tribes build their houses on bamboo platform or 'machan'. The Lotha's method is a short of compromise. He covers the floor of the machan with earth.[101]

In comparision to the Angami houses, the houses of the Lotha and Rengma Nagas are not nearly so large, well-built and substantial, the material is also not so good, and bamboo is used more freely instead of wood. The houses of the Lothas are distinguished from all others by their peculiarly-shaped roof. On the ridge of the usual thatched roof, and raised from it, is another small thatched roof or ridge, which projects some feet over each gable end, which looks like a provision for the escape of smoke and for ventilation; but it is unlikely that such a thing was ever thought of this tribe.[102] The Sema and Angami houses are not arranged in regular streets within the village site, but each individual appears to put his own house where he finds it most convenient to do so, due regard being had to the fact that the houses must for purposes of defence be not too widely scattered. The houses of Sema chiefs are distinguished by their extra size.[103]

The typical Kachcha Naga house differs from that of any other tribe. The front of their house bears the appearance of a high arch pointed at the top. The doorway is in the centre. The roof slopes down and back from the apex of the arch, which is sometimes as high as 20 feet, until it touches, or nearly touches, the ground. In the same manner the thatch on either side is brought down with a steep slope either actually on to the ground or, as is more commonly the case, to a foot or a foot and a half. The spaces on the sides and in front are planked in. As in most cases, there are two rooms inside the house, a sitting and eating, and a cooking and store-room.[104]

The traditional Naga houses had no latrines and people had to go to nearby forests to answer the call of nature. In case of the children, very old or sick persons or untimely motion any convenient place was chosen near the house and the same was cleaned by the pigs immediately.

The Nagas used locally available material for the construction of their houses. Mostly, thatch was used for roofing. Slate was used in the Khiamngan and Pochury areas and thatch or shingle by the Tangkhuls for roofing. Nails were rarely used as cane and creepers were readily available for the purpose. The house was abandoned when struck by the lightening or in case of 'apotia' death.

Several rituals and ceremonies accompanied house construction. Apart from the site selection ceremony, rituals were performed practically at every stage of the house construction.[105]

The Nagas Society, like many others in the country, rewarded head-hunters, givers of feasts and stone pullers[106] giving them certain privileges. One was able to recognise them by seeing their dresses, ornaments and houses.

The attitude of the people also differed from tribe to tribe. As for example, the attitude of the Konyaks, Lothas and the Aos towards their ageing parents differed considerably.[107] The standard of morals also varied considerably.[108]

REFERENCES

1. B.B. Kumar, 'Nagaland: An Overview', *Journal of Social Research*, Vol. XXVII, No. 1, p. 4; Ranchi (March 1984).
2. Hokishe Sema, *Emergence of Nagaland,* New Delhi (1986), p. 2.
3. Kumar, *op. cit.*, p 2.
4. J.P. Mills, *The Ao Nagas*, p. 1, n. 1.
5. E.T. Dalton, *Descriptive Ethnology of Bengal* , 1872, p. 38, cited in *The Nagas in the Nineteenth Century,* Verrier Elwin, p. 400.

6. Kumar, B.B., *Origin of the Word Naga,* Highlander, Vol. 1, No. 1, Kohima, March 1973, pp. 31-34.
7. Roy Burman, B.K., *Demographic and Socio-Economic Profiles of the Hill Areas of North-East India,* Census of India, 1961, New Delhi, p. 98.
8. Elwin, Verrier, *Nagaland*, NEFA Administration, Shillong (1961), p. 4.
9. Soppit, C.A., *A Short Account of the Kachcha (Empeo) Tribe in the North Cachar Hills* (1985), Reprint, p. 1.
10. Hokishe Sema, *op. cit.*, p. 2.
11. Dalton, *Descriptive Ethnology of Bengal.*
12. Hutton, *The Angami Nagas,* p. 4.
13. Roy Burman, *op. cit.*, p. 99.
14. Kumar, B.B., *The Thinker*, Vol. XII, No. 3, 4; Kohima (August, November, 1984), p. 41.
15. J.H. Hutton, *op. cit.*, p. 21.
16. Kaupuis are called Kabui now.
17. Elwin, *Nagas in the Nineteenth Century*, p. 459.
18. *Ibid.*, p. 20.
19. Hutton, *op. cit.*, p. 20.
20. *Ibid.*, p. 21.
21. Elwin, *The Nagas in the Nineteenth Century,* pp. 301-02.
22. *Ibid.*, p. 323.
23. *Ibid.*, p. 372.
24. *Ibid.*, p. 352.
25. Mills, *The Lotha Nagas*, p. XIII.
26. Elvin, *The Nagas in the Nineteenth Century*, p. 357.
27. *Ibid.*, p. 419.
28. *Ibid.*, p. 468.
29. *Ibid.*, p. 466.
30. *Ibid.*, p. 403.
31. Hutton, *op. cit.*, p. 377.
32. Hutton, *Introduction of 'The Lotha Nagas'*, p. XXII.
33. *Ibid.*
34. Majung is the name of the Changs.
35. Quoted in *A Brief Historical Account of Nagaland* by Alemchiba, pp. 117-18.
36. Mills, *The Lotha Nagas,* p. 6.
37. John Butler, in *The Nagas in the Nineteenth Century* by Verrier Elwin, p. 309.
38. *Nagas in the Nineteenth Century*, p. 460.
39. John Butler, cited in *The Nagas in the Nineteenth Century*, p. 309.
40. *Ibid.*
41. *Ibid.*, p. 308.
42. Elwin, *Nagas in the Nineteenth Century,* pp. 320-21.
43. *Ibid.*, pp. 64-65.
44. *Ibid.*, p. 351.
45. *Ibid.*, p. 372.

46. Hodson, T.C., *The Naga Tribes of Manipur,* pp. 21-22.
47. *Ibid.*, pp. 22-26.
48. *Ibid.*, p. 27.
49. *Ibid.*
50. Hutton, *The Angami Nagas*, p. 377.
51.
    Alemchiba Ao, *Arts and Crafts of Nagaland.*
52. Hutton, *The Sema Nagas*, p. 49, footnote.
53. Hutton, *The Angami Nagas*, pp.177-78.
54. *Ibid.*, p. 378.
55. Mills, *The Rengma Nagas*, p. 41.
56. *Ibid.*, pp. 32-33.
57. *Ibid.*, p. 33.
58. Mills, *The Lotha Nagas*, p. 15; *The Ao Nagas,* p. 55.
59. Mills, *The Ao Nagas,* p. 44.
60. *Ibid.*, p. 49.
61. Mills, *The Rengma Nagas*, p. 87.
62. Mills, *The Lotha Nagas*, p. 16.
63. *Ibid.*, p. 17.
64. *Ibid.*, pp. 24-25.
65. Hutton, *The Angami Nagas*, p. 29.
66. *Ibid.*, p. 22.
67. Hodson, *op. cit.*, pp. 27-30.
68. Hutton, *op. cit.*, p. 233.
69. *Ibid.*, p. 353.
70. *Ibid.*, p. 385.
71. *Ibid.*, p. 371.
72. *Ibid.*, p. 376.
73. *Ibid.*, pp. 382-83.
74. *Ibid.*, pp. 379, 382.
75. *Ibid.*, p. 25.
76. John Butler, cited in *The Nagas in the Nineteenth Century,* p. 308.
77. Verrier, Elwin, *op. cit.*, p. 351.
78. *Ibid.*, p. 372.
79. Hutton, *The Angami Nagas*, p. 36.
80. *Ibid.*, Note 1.
81. Soppit, C.A.; *A Short Account of the Kachcha Naga (Empeo) Tribe in the North Cachar Hills*, 1885, pp. 1-20.
82. Ganguli, Milada, *Pilgrimage to the Nagas*, pp. 206-07.
83. Davis, A.W., *Census of India*, 1891, Assam, Vol. 1, pp. 246-48; cited in Elwin, The Nagas in the Nineteenth Century, p. 373.
84. Brown, R., *Statistical Account of the Native State of Manipur,* 1873; cited in Elwin's *The Nagas in the Nineteenth Century,* p. 373.
85. Elwin, *The Nagas in the Nineteenth Century*, p. 484.
86. Kumar, B.B., *The Tribal Societies of India,* p. 97.
87. *Ibid.*, p. 98.
88. *Nagas in the Nineteenth Century,* pp. 65-66.
89. Mills, J.P., *The Rengma Nagas*, p. 45.

90. *Ibid.*
91. Kumar, B.B., *Society and Culture in a Corner of Nagaland*, p. 3.
92. Mills, *The Lotha Nagas*, p. 96.
93. *Ibid.*, p. XXXIII; Hutton, *The Angami Nagas*, p. 187.
94. Mills, *The Lotha Nagas*, p. 5.
95. *Ibid.*
96. *Ibid.*, pp.6, 126.
97. *Ibid.*, p. 5.
98. *Ibid.*
99. *Ibid.*, pp. 5-6.
100. *Ibid.*, p. 4.
101. Mills, *The Lotha Nagas*, p. XXX; H. Bareh, *Nagaland District Gazetteer*, Kohima district, pp. 81-82.
102. *Nagas in the Nineteenth Century*, pp. 284, 269, 335.
103. *Ibid.*, p. 373.
104. *Ibid.*, p. 412.
105. Bareh, *op. cit.*, p. 82.
106. Mills, *The Lotha Nagas*, p. 14.
107. *Ibid.*, pp. 19-20.
108. *Ibid.*, p. 19.

3

THE NAGA IDENTITY FORMATION

The tribal people of our North-Eastern fringe were called 'Noga' by their neighbours of the Brahmaputra valley. The origin of the word 'Naga' is obscure and it is variously derived from different words by different scholars.[1]

The Nagas did not have a generic term for themselves. A Naga used to identify himself by giving the name of his village. Sometimes specific names were given to a group of villages.[2] Even as late as 1954, Verrier Elwin found people calling themselves as Nagas today to be unaware of the term 'Naga'.[3] The Nagas do not have common legends of origin and migration. They differ in their social structure, village polity, physical features, temperament, dress, hair style, tattooing, setting of villages, housing pattern, mode of agriculture, etc. The traditions of the origin of the Naga tribes cannot be reconciled with a homogeneous origin. Even different clans of a single tribe may not have traditions of homogeneous origin. Migration has taken place almost from every direction. There are legends of origin from stones, caves, lakes and the sky. The mode of the disposal of the dead, belief in life after death, etc. vary from tribe to tribe.[4]

There is so much linguistic plurality among the Nagas that different sections of a tribe or different villages of the same tribe, and even wife and the husband at a time speak different languages.[5]

A very marked point of distinction among Nagas is the use of terraced cultivation. Among the tribes practising jhuming, there is a marked difference in sowing rice. Unlike other tribes, taro is the staple food of the Konyaks, and not rice. The custom of erecting monoliths is closely associated with terraced cultivation. There are other miscellaneous considerations also which suggest the diversity of the Naga tribes, such as the method of reaping the crop. Whereas most of the Nagas use reaping hook, the Semas, like Karens and Garos, use their hand only, striping the grain from the stalk straight into the basket. It is a most painful method of reaping to avoid threshing.[6]

The gennas observed by different Naga tribes also show that there is so little similarity among them.[7] Different food taboos are observed by different Naga tribes. The Nagas of the Maram group forbid pork.[8] The migratory habits of the tribes differ. Semas migrate and found new villages. Other tribes, like Lothas[9], are non-migratory. The oath-taking by Aos and Western Nagas differ.[10] Angamis and Konyaks, though geographically apart, exhibit some resembling traits.[11] The Chang and Konyak Nagas reside far away from the Bodo and Kuki tribes, but their languages, in fact, reflect noticeable commonalities.[12]

Most of the Nagas believe in the souls of the dead inhabiting butterflies or other insects. They also believe in an existence in the future world where the dead go and live. Most of the tribes place it underground and point towards some mountain from which the underworld is approached. The Semas believe that the spirits of the good dead go to the East and those of the bad ones to the West. According to the Angami belief, the souls of the dead who have conformed to the best standard of life, spend their future existence in company of the ancestors or creatrix of all life in a sky world.[13]

As mentioned earlier, the village polity and the social structure of the Naga tribes differ considerably and suggest a diversity of origin. There are traces of a dual division crossed by a triple one in more than one tribe. This indicated the division of the tribe into three elements, either as three separate groups or as two primary groups, one of which splitting into two again to make it three. The two linguistic groups—Mongsen and Chongli—and three phratries exist side by side in the same Ao village. The Chami phratry among the Aos has inferior status. There are two linguistic groups—Thendu and Thenkoh—among the Konyaks, side by side with three social divisions. Two linguistic divisions exist among Angamis, Lothas and the Western Rengmas also. The Thekronoma or Cheroma division of the Angamis is also known as Solhima, which means "alien" or "stranger". Cherhechima division among the Memi tribe is regarded as socially inferior and other Memis did not intermarry with them. Ung clan among the Chang Nagas is the priestly clan. One of this clan must be in every Chang village. But this clan was usually spoken of with contempt, and therefore, Hutton presumed them to represent the conquered population aquainted with the gods of the soil, at any rate in the Chang area.[14] Similar inference was drawn about the Chami phratry among the Aos, as mentioned elsewhere. The Naga tribes also have legends of clans descended from indigenous women out of caves or wild men caught in the jungle and tamed.[15] The colour of the Nagas varies from red to brown red and even dark colour.[16] The features vary considerably from Mongoloid to even Negrito type.[17] Cephalic indices, as per the available data, suggest connection between Aos, Manipuris, Ahoms, and perhaps some other sub-Himalayan tribes. It might be due to common infusion of Tai blood.[18] Konyaks also have the admixture of Shan blood.[19]

It is evident from the above-mentioned description that there is considerable ethnic diversity among the Nagas. The said diversity extends even from village to household level. Hutton's remark in this connection is worth-quoting:

> "It would be impossible to give any general description of the type of the Angami features, as it varies from village to village and even from house to house in a remarkable degree. The flattened nose and slightly oblique eye of a decidedly Mongolian type may be seen side by side with a straightness of eyes and nose that might be purely Aryan."[20]

This kind of extreme ethnic diversity among the Nagas has resulted due to mixing of ethnic elements from diverse sources, during successive migrations. W.C. Smith (The Ao Naga Tribe) has listed 14 physical and cultural traits—head-hunting, dormitory for young men, house on piles, disposal of dead on platforms, tribals marriage customs, betel chewing, aversion to milk, tattooing, lack of political organisation, double cylinder forge, loin-loom, hexagonal shields, residence in hilly regions and jhum cultivation of Tibeto-Burman. These are not the common markers in the case of the Nagas. Many traits have all India, and even global presence. The markers of ethnic identity, given by Anthony Smith in his definition of ethnic community, are "a named human population with a myth of common ancestry, shared memories and cultural elements; link to a historic territory or homeland; and a measure of solidarity."[21] The markers, according to Ghai, are langauge, race, religion and colour.[22] As discussed above, and elsewhere in this book, the Nagas do not have the myth of common ancestry, shared memories and cultural elements, and a common language. Historically, their territory has linkages with Ahoms/Brahmaputra valley,[23] Meithei kingdom,[24] Kachari kingdom[25] and Singphos[26]. Traditional religion has already been abandoned; they have adopted Christianity. They lacked any measure of solidarity; numerous villages and tribes continuously fought wars against each other.[27] They have diverse racial elements and differ in physical features and colour.

Too much intra-Naga ethnic and cultural differences, blurred distinguishing markers between Nagas and non-Naga tribes, loose applicability of the term, lack of historical depth of the Naga identity in spite of the empty rhetoric and their obsession about history and Nagas' confusion about their own identity have not come in the way of Naga identity formation. It is a case of recent, but stable identity formation. The Nagas not only did not use the term, but even resented to be called Naga.[28] The Nagas do not differ much from other tribes of the North-East and "if not impossible, it is exceedingly difficult to propound any test by which a Naga tribe can be distinguished from other Assam or Burma tribes, which are not Nagas."[29] Due to such blurred distinction, the term "Naga" continued to be loosely used, even for Kacharis, Kukis, Abors,[30] Karbi, Nepali,[31] Khamti and Singpho.[32] Kukis, against whom the NSCN(IM) is waging almost a war, were included as a Naga tribe even in well-publicised Simon Commission Memorandum.[33] Anals are a Kuki-Chin tribe,[34] but they are claiming to be Naga today. Similar is the case of the smaller groups like Lamkhang and

Monsang.[35] The names of the tribes and their number varies from Census to Census and from author to author. Even Isak Swu, Chairman, NSCN(IM) gives different figures about the area of inhabitation and population of the Nagas.[36] Thus Naga identity continues to be a fluid identity even today. Dr. Kumar Suresh Singh, former Director General of Anthropological Survey of India, has aptly remarked: "Perceptions appear to be amorphous, fluid, changing all the time. Therefore lists vary from Census to Census and no two lists are exactly comparable."[37]

The Eastern Naga tribes of Myanmar have closer affiliations with the Kachins and NSCN(IM) had to forcibly establish themselves amongst the Naga tribes in some areas, as at Kesan Chanlam, and convert them to Christianity. The book of Bertil Lintner, who has pointed out the fact, has been reportedly banned by the NSCN(IM).[38] The forcible conversion of the Nagas to Christianity is also reported from Arunachal Pradesh.[39] According to Dr. Xavier P. Mao, a teacher in North-Eastern Hill University, and himself a Naga from Manipur, "Christianity along with English Education have played a very significant role in the Naga society in their struggle for a sovereign and independent Nagalim.[40]

The Government of British India brought about half a dozen Naga tribes under single administrative unit. This was beginning of a change from hundreds of village republics to a single administrative unit. Merger of Naga Hills district with Tuensang and elevation of the merged unit to statehood further consolidated their identity. The statehood was responsible for extensive development input. These factors consolidated Naga unity. The Britishers kept them isolated, planted seeds of separation in the minds of some of them, and really planned separation of the hills of India and Burma into separate crown colony. A sense of fear was also injected in the minds of unsophisticated Nagas by the British officers and the Phizoites. Therefore, it is fair to conclude that the present Naga identity formation is of recent origin moulded by conviction to a common religion Christianity, English education, administrative measures like creation of districts and State and recent economic developmental activities. Any belief or claim that its rooted in history and anthropology will be contrary to the facts.

REFERENCES

1. See chapter on "Nagas : an Overview" in this book.
2. Verrier Elwin, *Nagas in the Nineteenth Century,* p. 47.
3. Verrier Elwin, *Nagaland,* Shillong, 1961.
4. Materials given in different chapters of this book.
5. The Tangkhuls avoid marriage in some villages due to unintelligibility of languages; *vide* Nagas of Manipur, T.C. Hodson, pp. 19, 85.
6. Mills, *The Lotha Nagas,* pp. XXVIII-XXIX.
7. Hodson, *op. cit.*, p. 166.
8. *Ibid.*, pp. 84, 81.
9. Mills, *The Lotha Nagas,* p. XXXV.
10. Hutton, *The Angami Nagas,* p. 374.
11. *Ibid.*, p. 386.
12. Mills, *The Lotha Nagas,* p. XXXV, Grierson, *Linguistic Survey of India.*
13. *Ibid.*, pp. XXXIII-XXXIV.
14. *Ibid.*, pp. XXX-XXXII.
15. *Ibid.*, p. XXI.
16. Bareh, *Nagaland District Gazetteer,* Kohima district, p. 20.
17. Mills, *The Lotha Nagas,* p. XXIII.
18. *Ibid.*
19. Hutton, *The Angami Nagas,* p. 384.
20. *Ibid.*, p. 21.
21. Anthony D. Smith, *Nationalism in the Twentieth Century,* Martin Robertson Oxford, 1979, p. viii.
22. Ghai, *Autonomy and Ethnicity,* p. 4; quoted by Lt. Gen. (Retd.) Sushil K. Pillai, Ethnicity, Autonomy and Governance; *Faultline,* Vol. 10, p. 31.
23. J.P. Mills, *The Ao Nagas,* p. 5, *The Lotha Nagas,* p. 1; Gait, *The History of Assam,* p. 308; Hutton, *The Angami Nagas,* p. 13.
24. Maos, Tangkhuls, Rongmei, etc. were already the subjects of the Manipur king before the arrival of the British.
25. Zemi Nagas of Cachar were the subjects of the Kachari Rajas before the arrival of the British.
26. Eastern Nagas near Patkai were the subjects of the Singphos.
27. Any book on the Nagas/monographs are full of the details of intra-Naga feuds and raids and counter-raids between the villages even of the same tribe (*vide* Hutton's *Angami Nagas,* pp. 7, 12, 17; Mills, *Lotha Nagas,* p. 20. The word for enemy in Lotha Language is Uri, which is also the name of the Ao Nagas in their language.
28. Hokishe Sema, *The Emergence of Nagaland,* p. 2.
29. Hutton, *op. cit.*, p. 4.
30. Dalton, *Descriptive Ethnology of Bengal.*
31. *Faultlines,* Vol. 14, p. 73.
32. Charles Chasie, *The Naga Imbroglio,* p. 19.
33. *Vide* Annexure 1 of this book.
34. *Vide* Grierson's *Linguistic Survey of India.*
35. *Faultline,* Vol. 10, p. 27.

36. *Ibid.*, Vol. 3, pp. 43-45.
37. Kumar Suresh Singh, *People of India*, Vol. 1, Introduction, p. 40; Calcutta, 1992.
38. Bertil Lintner's book, *Land of Jade*, Kiskadel, 1990; *vide* Sushil K. Pillai, *Anatomy of an Insurgency, Ethnicity and Identity in Nagaland*, in *Faultline*, Vol. 3, pp. 43-45; New Delhi, 1999.
39. *Tehelka* Special Report, July 10, 2004.
40. Proceedings of the Seminar on *Foundations of Naga Peoplehood: Roadmaps*; Centre for Democracy and Tribal Studies, Kohima, 2003.

4

ORIGIN AND MIGRATION OF THE NAGA TRIBES

Legends of Origin

Nagas have numerous legends of origin and dispersal of tribes. According to Ao Naga legend, their ancestors came out of the earth from six stones, called Lungterok (lung=stone; terok=six) at Chungliyimti village, located on the right bank of the Dikhu river in Sangtam Naga area opposite to the Longsa village. According to their belief, three stones were males and three were females. Pongen and Lungkam phratries claim origin from one of the female stones and the Chami phratry from one of the male ones. The Phom Nagas also believe in Lungterok origin of their tribe. The Ao Nagas believe that Semas and Changs also emerged from Lungterok, but the Sema and Chang Nagas do not agree to the legend of their common origin with the Aos from Lungterok.[1] Sangtams Nagas also emerged from the earth at Lungterok and stayed together with the Phoms in the same village forming separate *khels* (sections). J.P. Mills has written about their separation in the following words:

> "One day the Sangtams proposed a mock fight, each side to use bamboo spears, and plantain leaves instead of shields. The Phoms agreed, and being simple honest souls (they have changed since), observed the conditions, while the Sangtams covered real shields with plantain leaves. The natural result was that the Phoms had many casualties and the Sangtams none. Disliking such treacherous people as neighbours the Phoms migrated to their present country."[2]

Mills has mentioned about an exactly similar story of fight between two Sema clans during their migration.[3] Mongsen were the first to emerge from earth followed by the Chonglis, who settled at Kubok and Chongliyimti villages respectively. They fought war among them; and forced Mongsens to come to Chongliyimti and settle in a separate *khel* in that village resulting into their long-lasting partnership, migration and spread over in the present Ao area.[4]

According to Kezakenoma legend, the ancestors of the Angamis, Semas and Lotha Nagas were brothers, who lived together with their parents in Kezakenoma village in Kheja area. They, in turn, used to spread paddy on a big flat stone in which a spirit used to inhabit, as a result of which the paddy used to become double in load. On a particular day, the brothers failed to decide the turn for spreading rice resulting into bitter fight. The parents were afraid fearing bloodshed. They broke eggs on the stone and set it on fire; the stone burst with thunderous sound. The spirit came out of the stone and its virtue was lost. The three brothers dispersed in three directions after that. The parents remaining there, became the ancestors of the Kheja Nagas.[5] The legend with slight modification, is shared by the Angamis, Semas, Rengmas, Lothas and the Maos.[6]

Here, it needs mention that Kezakenoma legend is unknown to the Aos[7]. Similarly, Lungterok legend was not known to the Angamis and other western Nagas. According to a legend, certain sections of Rengma, Sema and Lotha Nagas stayed together below the new township of Tsemenyu, where a stone-slab, placed to commemorate their stay together, still exists.[8] Kepezoma and Kepepfuma, the two divisions of the Angami Nagas, according to a legend, descended from two brothers who came out of the earth. The Angamis do not specify the place of happening, but they believe that the prints of the hand, feet and the knees of their ancestors may still be found in front of the hole from which they emerged. They pointed towards Mao and the country beyond as the place of their origin.[9] It needs mention that the words of the priests of Mao and Mekroma (Maikei) villages were necessary for fixing regular Angami festival dates. It is also believed that Maikel stone was the place where ancestors of the Angamis emerged from the earth.[10] According to yet another Angami Naga legend, three persons emerged from a lake. The first one, the ancestor of the Maos and the Marams went southwards; the second, the ancestor of the Kacha Nagas, went westwards. The third one did not go anywhere, he settled there and became the ancestor of the Angamis.[11]

An Angami Naga legend points towards the common origin of the Nagas and the Teprima (Indians). According to that legend, both are the descendants of Ukepenopfu and her husband, who had very long moustache and beard reaching down to his feet. He was very wise and was living in a vessel. One day, the elder son, who was the ancestor of the Nagas, saw his father and was frightened to see him. He ran away from them and thus was unable to receive wisdom and knowledge from his father. The younger son, who was the ancestor of the Indians remained with his parents, received education from his father and thereby became wise. This story explains why Nagas remained poor in knowledge and wisdom in comparison to the Indians in spite of their common origin.[12] A similar story of the Angami Nagas, pointing towards the common origin of the Nagas and the plainsmen explains why the plainsmen are so numerous and the Nagas are not. According to that legend, the Nagas and the plainsmen are descendants of the two brothers and their followers. The two brothers and their followers used branches of Chombu and Chomu trees for lightening their paths during their dispersal. The Chombu tree gives light for several days; the brother using it for blazing the path had many followers who travelled for many days and reached the plains. The ancestor of the Nagas used Chomu tree for blazing the path. It burnt very fast, gave light for very short time; the followers were few in number and they remained behind in the hills.[13] The Memi equivalent of Ukepenopfu is Jilimasa. She was produced by the god Ura. A cloud came from the south, had connection with her and she produced a god and then a tiger. The cloud came three more times and she gave birth to three beings, named Asapu, Tothoh and Kepi. Kepi stayed there and became the ancestor of the Haus (A Manipuri term for the Nagas), Tuthoh and Asapu went to the Manipur valley and to the west and became the ancestors of the Meitheis (Manipuris) and the Mayangs (Bangalis/ Indians) respectively.[14] This legend, apart from pointing towards wider Naga linkages has also element of totemism.

The Chang Nagas emerged from earth at Changsang (homeland of the Changs) or Changsang Mongko village. Changsang Mongko lies about 15 kilometres north-east of Tuensang town in a deeply forested area between Tuensang and Hakchang villages. The Changsang legend informs about the origin, migration, clan formation based on different functions of the Changs and their links with the Konyaks and Phoms. As the tradition says, the Changs during their migration from the east, met a dwarf tribe, called 'Shumpak Mopakshou'. When asked, 'who are your parents?', one of them replied that 'we are our parents' and broke a pastle with his two hands. They came upto Lanyyong river near Noklak and then to Changsang, their first settlement. At Changsang, their population multiplied and the four clans based on the division of labour were formed. The Changsang legend is shared by the Changs, Phoms and the Konyaks. There was migration of Konyaks and Phoms from Changsang to the north, and of Changs to the Langa village. The people from Tiso Tiyong came and settled with them at Langa. The Legend is shared by the Changs and the Yimchungrus. Tuensang was peopled by the migration from Langa and Changsang. According to yet another tradition, the descendants of two brothers settled it and the villages north and south of Tuensang.[15]

Langa suffered due to internal strife and was destroyed. The Chang tradition also mentions about the great flood and the dispersal of the tribe to all directions. This provides basis to their thinking that once they lived together with Yimchungrus, Sangtams, Konyaks and Phoms, and all at that time were one tribe. They developed different tribal traits only after their dispersal and isolated living.[16] Hutton has also mentioned about a legend of felling of rubber tree and the dispersal and separation of the Changs, Semas, Yimchungrus, Sangtams, Aos, Khiamngans and Konyak tribes and some clans of the Changs.[17]

The Wancho Nagas have a legend, according to which a Wancho chief originated from a red gourd. Aju Ajong (a god-like man; also called Piju Ngowang) was roaming once in a forest, which was his domain, and he found three red gourds one after the other. He found a pair of man and women in each of the first and the third; and a pair of men in the second one and told them to go and get multiplied.[18]

According to another tradition, a girl was fertilized by wind and the Wancho tribe originated. The Khimamngan Nagas of Wui village believed that their parents, who were brother, and sister, came down from the sky on that place. It needs mention that Wui, among the Nagas, is the only village where clan endogamy is practised. Tangsas seek their origin in Masoi Sinrapum hill, somewhere towards the east.[19]

Hodson, while discussing the traditions of origin of the Tangkhul Nagas of the North East Manipur has categorised them into three groups. He writes:

> "In case of the Tangkhuls the traditions as to their origin resolve themselves into at least three groups. In the first group are the traditions which connect them with the valley and derive them thence as emigrants on account of the heat and mosquitoes. According to the second group of traditions, the village of Hundung (which must be distinguished from Tangkhul Hundung) is the centre of their dispersion, and the stories declare that they sprang from immigrants from the village of Maikel Tunggam (a village which is also the traditional home of the common ancestors of the Quasi Angami tribes in the Mao group). The third set of traditions refers to a period rather later and mainly deals with the growth of new villages and their establishment by emigrants from older villages which suffered from an excess of population."[20]

He further writes:

> "The second group of tradition affords a link with the general tradition which makes Nagas, Kukis and Manipuris descended from a common ancestor, who had three sons who became the progenitors of these tribes.[21] The Mao Naga variant of this Tangkhul legend connects the hill tribes, Naga and Kuki with the Manipuris.[22] The legend of the three brothers becoming the progenitors of the Kukis, Nagas and the Manipuris, coupled with the fact that they migrated in comparatively recent times, under the pressure of the advancing tribes from the south, from sites in the south-east of the valley beyond Moirang to their present homes.[23] According to a tradition, the Kabuis/ Roungmei Nagas claim their origin from Thungching mountain towards the south of the Manipur valley and that they are presently occupying the village sites once occupied by the southern tribes, who are, they say, the elder branch of the family of which they themselves are the middle and Munniporees the younger branch."[24]

Quoireng Nagas claim that they were driven from their homes in the north-east by the people of Maram.[25] Marams, on the other hand, are said to have had their origin from immigrants from the west.[26] Not only the ancestors of the Marams came from the west, but the two were the only survivors of the great flood which destroyed all mankind except them. Some other elements of interest in their case are that their "exogamous principle is founded on divine ordinance; they forbid flesh of the pig and thereby "have the almost totemistic connection of an animal ancestor with the prohibition against the flesh of the animal"; and as their marriage takes place in the jungle, and not in the village or the house, it is intimately connected with the marital genna.[27]

In many cases, a tribe has more than one legend/tradition of origin. A section of Maring tribe has origin at a place called 'Haubum Maruk' in Imphal. Another section has its origin at Leisang Kong village in the Manipur valley some 7-8 miles south of the capital. Dr. Brown, as quoted by T.C. Hodson, however, gives another account of the origin of the Marings. He wrote: "The origin of the Marings is thus given by themselves. 'We originally came out of the earth near the eastern foot of the eastern Heerok range, but in the Kubbo valley, in the higher ground immediately under the hills at a place named Mungsa. Seven men and seven women thus emerged. At this time, women and men wore the same cloths (the *dhoti* or cloth round the loin is to this day identical in both sexes, though worn differently).[28]

Both Tangkhuls and Marings give different versions of their origin. As stated earlier, the Tangkhuls legend connects them with Manipur valley. It declares that "they sprang from a stone in the police lines, which curiously enough is also claimed by a section of the Maring Nagas; the southern neighbours of the Tangkhuls, as their place of origin. They left the valley because the heat and mosquitoes made life there impossible."[29] The fire, they carried with them was extinguished on the way and a Deity taught them to make it from stone. According to another tradition, the Tangkhuls came out of a cave in earth at a place called Murringphy in the hills, about four days' journey north-east of the Manipur valley. A large tiger, watching them coming out one by one, used to devour them. They, however, managed to come in large number by a stratagem; the tiger ran away after that.[30]

The Angami Nagas came to their present site from the south-east; the place of their dispersal being Kezakenoma village of the Kheza tribe. But the Angami tradition points towards further south to a village, in the Tangkhul country, known to them as Piwhema. However, unmistakable traces of terraced cultivation found far to the south in Mizoram points towards further south still as the possible places from which they immigrated. Puchatsuma clan of the Angamis of Kohima village, like Khoirao Nagas, came from the west, while another clan of that village claims migration from the south-west direction from the present day Zeliangruong country. As discussed earlier, the Angami legend claims origin from the ancestress, a spirit in the sky, as well as from the ancestors emerging from the bowels of the earth at Mekrima.[31] The Rengmas migrated from the Kheza country in the south, with the Angamis and Lothas, throwing out the Naked Rengmas eastwards to Meluri, and ultimately sending the bigger portion of the tribe westwards to the Karbi Anglong.[32] A section of the Lothas, however, points very definitely to the snows of the Himalayas seen far to the north-west as the home of their ancestors."[33]

> The traditions of Migration of the Sema Nagas, like other Western Nagas tribes, point to the south as the direction of their immigration. Their ancestors, according to them, sprang from Japvo (Tukahu) mountain, and they claim that Semas migrated from Swemi or Semi village near Kezabama. The village, though retaining the Sema as the domestic language, has adopted the Angami dress and is surrounded now by the Angami villages.[34] Hutton, on the basis of their links with the Khoirao tribe, suggests western origin of the part of the Sema tribe and their link with the Bodos. Hutton has compared the numerals and vocabularies of Khoirao of Khongde and Ngari with that of the Sema, Kachari and Garo languages, apart from some other facts and has drawn positive conclusion to show the western linkage of the Sema.[35]

As stated earlier, the Ao Nagas claim trans-Dikhu origin. Their own word for the tribe is Aor (Ao is a current mispronunciation of Aor, meaning 'those who came' across Dikhu). The term for Sangtams, Changs, Phoms and Konyaks is Mirir; meaning, 'those who did not come'.[36] Though, bulk of the Ao tribe claims an autochthonous origin at Chongliyimti, they claim a part origin from the plains to the north-west. This is also the case with the Konyaks. Mills have written:

> From Tamlu northwards there are the various Konyak tribes, whose traditions of origin at least include an ascription of their origin to the hills to the north and the migration from the plains in the west or north-west as well, though others, perhaps with Singpho affinities, reached their present country from the north-east, while one or two Konyak villages, indistinguishable from the Konyaks generally in culture, claim an origin from the country to the south of them at present occupied by Aos.[37] Some of the Konyaks derive their origin from the north-east or east.[38] The Sangtams claim to a south-eastern origin. The Northern Sangtams, as mentioned by Mills, "merely point to the south, but the Southern Sangtams derive their origin from the Chindwin valley to the south-east of them, and have a vague tradition that their tribe has become separated into two parts of which one went apparently west, while remnants are believed to exist in the Chindwin valley still. It seems likely that the part of the tribe that went westwards may be represented today in the Lotha tribe. Who have a similar if more definite tradition about the splitting of their tribe into two parts, of which one stayed behind at the time of migration."[39]

Thus Nagas have received ethnic elements from all the directions, and as Mills has observed, "First of all we have the Naga traditions of origin themselves, indicating, as one would expect to find, almost all the points of the compass."[40]

The Sema tribe during their migration have been influenced by and have influenced and absorbed other tribes in it. Their languages are most closely related to Kheza language. There is a close superficial relation between the Semas and Chakrima Angamis. This is, because, 'a number of villages now rèckoned Chekrama are largely of Sema origin, the customs, dress, and languages of the Chekrama Angamis having been adopted as a result of contact with and domination by that tribe. These villages, being bilingual, speak Sema and Chakrima languages indifferently.'[41] The Semas, in many villages, have considerable mixture of the blood of other tribes. Hutton writes:

> "The Semas of Lazemi, on the other hand, and some other villages in the Dayang Valley, seem to have a fairly strong mixture of Tengima Angami and, in some cases, of Rengma blood, which has influenced their languages and customs so much as to make them noticeably different from the genuine Sema. There is a decided admixture of Sangtam and even of Ao blood in the northern Semas, and a very considerable mixture of Tukomi Sangtam to the east, while in the north-east corner a little Chang and Yachumi blood has been introduced. The result of contact with these tribes may also be seen to a certain extent in the customs observed by the Semas and in their songs and dances. Generally speaking, however, the Sema is predominant in mixed villages, and though in some way very receptive, it is his language and polity which usually prevail. It is only in the case of one or two villages on the Chekrama border that he has fallen under the influence of another tribe so far to adopt its customs and language in place of his own."[42]

Such phenomena is not restricted to the Sema tribe alone. There are other examples also of the same in Naga inhabited areas. Aos have Chongli, Mongsen and Changki as distinct "language groups" undoubtedly representing different waves of immigrants speaking different dialects. Then there used to be 'Sangpur' dialect which became obsolete some eighty years ago and was spoken in the Sangpur *khel* of the Longsa village. Yacham and Yong speak a dialect resembling Chongli, but follow Phom or Konyak customs to a great extent.[43] Mills has written about the identity crisis of the people faced under such situation. He wrote:

> "Yacham recently told me that they really did not know what they were—Aos would not recognize them as Aos and their trans-Dikhu neighbours would not accept them as kinsmen."[44]

Noksan and Longla villages have long been under Chang chiefs; have adopted Chang dress and customs, but an Ao dialect is current in them together with Chang dialect. It appeared that these villages lost their characteristic Ao customs.[45]

The tradition of migration of the Naga tribes, in a large number of cases is accompanied by the tradition of aggression followed by either pushing back the earlier settlers or subjugation and assimilation. The inferior clans/phratries in many cases belong to the subjugated sections of tribe.[46] Isangyongr, Nokrangr and Molungru are the three names for the early Konyak inhabitants of the Ao country.[47] Mills has mentioned about the internal wars during the process of migration of the Aos in their present habitat. According to him, Mongsens were the first to emerge from the earth at Chongliyimti, and they settled at Kubok, about whose existence the Changlis, who emerged next and settled at Chongliyimti, were blishfully ignorant. The Mongsen raiders from Kubok continually killed Chongli stragglers. Ultimately, the existence of Kubok and the secret of the loss of life of the Chonglis was found out by Shiluti, one of their great heroes. This resulted into war between the two villages leading to defeat of Kubok. Mongsen were forced to come to Chongliyimti and settle in a *khel* by the side of that of the Chonglis. A long co-partnership between the two communities and their migration across the Dikhu river started after that. All the villagers, except the few who were ancestors of the Sangpur *khel* of Longsa, crossed Dikhu and founded Lungkam, Ungma, Sutsu and Kabza, and then other villages. It needs mention that two of their earliest villages founded by them, Sangtamla and Kabza, had women rulers. Mokongtsu raiders destroyed Sangtamla and the female rule at Kabza was short-lived. In Kabza, however, the custom allowed to have a recognised woman representative of the female point of view, without being a member of the councils and having any privilege.[48] While moving towards the north-east on the Langbangkong range of hills, the Aos met Isangyongr people at Yongyimti; lived together with them for some time, but eventually the latter community moved on and now form the part of the population of Tamlu and Chota Kanching. The small monoliths, which the Konyaks continue to put up remained there on the sites abandoned by them.[49] Again the Aos had the war with the Nokrangr people, one of whose villages was situated at Nokrangrmangkoturong ("the place where Nokrangr hang their enemies' heads") on the present day Mongsenyimti land.

Nokpoyimchen, another traditional site was broken up by Lungkam. Natusu was located on Waromung land. The biggest and most famous village of the Nokrangr was at Alungtakiba, outside Lakhuni village, which was also attacked by Lungkam. A section of the refugees went to the Brahmaputra valley; another section entered the hills again and are said to be the forefathers of the Noklang clan of the Konyaks of Tamlu and Namsang. The former, as the Aos thought, became the ancestors of the Miri tribe. A third section, remaining in the hills, founded Nancham, usually known as Longsamtang by the Chonglis. The name 'Molungr' still survives in the names of Molungkong ridge and Molungyimchen village. It is said that the founders of Longchang village held them in high respect; bought the ridge for founding their village, but ultimately the two quarrelled and the former retreated to the north. A section of them, who were eventually driven to the plain of Brahmaputra valley crossed over to the hills to the north and settled there; another section returned in the Ao area and settled in Molungyimchen village. The latter represent Sanglichar clan there. A third section came back to the hills in the Konyak country. Nokrangr are said to have been potters; they shaved their heads at the sides and wore their hair in the bun at the back with a flat piece of bamboo stuck through, as the Konyaks used to do. Molungr, like Konyaks, were pot-makers and blacksmiths. It needs mention that pot-making is taboo in the Ao villages except in those of the Changki group, which are supposed to have a far larger proportion of Konyak blood.[50]

The Aos were also pressed from the south-west by the Lothas and later on the Semas. The Aos occupying the area as far south as Kileki stream were driven out by the invading Semas. The large Longsa village, consisting of the refugees from the southern Ao villages, was ready to settle on a newly cleared site to the north due to perpetual raiding of Seromi Semas, just at the time of the British annexation of the area. The oldest and biggest Ao village of Ungma had given up cultivation on Sema side at the time. Mokokchung was to follow it. Nankam was too big and strategically located and therefore a diffcult village for the Semas, anyway. At this point of time, the first Military police outpost was set up at Wokha and the Aos anticipating the end of war decided to stay on and thus were saved from being pushed to the north and west of Mokokchung. The expanding Semas, earlier were responsible for the separation of the Naked Rengmas from the western Rengmas and the ejection of the tribe from a strip of country running as far east as the Tizu. Kivikhu and one or two villages near the same, as Hutton has reported were known by the Angami Nagas as "Mezhamibagwe" or "formerly Rengma". The Sema migration stopped in the administered area after the advent of the British, but continued in the unadministered

Tuensang district. Like the Rengmas, the Semas separated the Sangtams into two parts by pushing a wedge and met the Yimchungru tribe.[51] The Sema migration in Dimapur took place after the formation of the state of Nagaland.

As is evident from the above-mentioned accounts, the issues related to the origin, migration and composition of the Naga tribes are complex ones. The intra-Naga conflicts and wars have also played its role in giving the Naga society the present shape. The observation of J.P. Mills, in this context, needs mention:

> "For Naga invaders do not as a rule obliterate their foes. More usually, after reducing the village which is their objective to a suitable frame of mind by repeated raides, they come and live in it as overlords, take wives from it, and gradually absorb it in their own community. Even if, the greater part of the invaded village does retreat out of range, as sometimes happens, some are almost sure either to remain or to creep back to an existence inglorious but secure."[52]

Some of the common features of the legends of origin and the traditions of migration of the Naga tribes need mention.

1. The perusal of the facts given above make it abundantly clear that not a single legend tradition of origin and migration is acceptable to or have currency among all the Naga tribes. In many cases, a single tribe has more than one legend of origin and tradition of migration.
2. The places of origin/dispersal of tribes vary from one group to another, if not from tribe to tribe.
3. The migration has taken place, practically from every directions; from the east, west, north and the south.
4. In many cases, there have been intra-Naga ethnic borrowing or assimilation leading to multiple legends/ traditions of origin and migration.

REFERENCES

1. Kumar, Dr. B.B., *The Tribal Societies of India;* New Delhi (1998), p. 122.
2. J.P. Mills, *The Ao Nagas,* Reprint, OUP, Bombay (1973), p. 6, n.1.
3. *Ibid.*
4. *Ibid.*

5. J.H. Hutton, *Angami Nagas;* Reprint, OUP, Bombay (1968), p. 19.
6. *Ibid.*, pp. 19-20
7. *Ibid.*, p. 375.
8. Kumar, *op. cit.*, p. 123.
9. Hutton, *op. cit*, p. 110.
10. *Ibid.*, pp. 7, 110.
11. Kumar, *op. cit.*, p. 123; Elwin, *The Nagas in the Nineteenth Century,* p. 459.
12. Hutton, *op. cit.*, pp. 260-61.
13. *Ibid.*, p. 261.
14. *Ibid.*, pp. 248-49.
15. Kumar, *op. cit.*, pp. 124-25.
16. *Ibid.*, pp. 125-27.
17. Hutton, *op. cit.*, pp. 381-82; Kumar, *op. cit.*, pp. 128-29.
18. L.R.N. Srivastva, *Wamchos*, p. 44.
19. Kumar, *op. cit.*, p. 123.
20. T.C. Hodson, *The Naga Tribes of Manipur;* Delhi, Low Price Publications, Reprint, 1996.
21. *Ibid.*, p. 9.
22. *Ibid.*, p. 11.
23. *Ibid.*, p. 16.
24. *Ibid.*, p. 14.
25. *Ibid.*
26. *Ibid.*, p. 162.
27. *Ibid.*, p. 13.
28. *Ibid.*, p. 15.
29. *Ibid.*, p. 10.
30. *Ibid.*
31. Mills, *The Lotha Nagas*, p. XX.
32. *Ibid.*, p. XXI.
33. *Ibid.*
34. *Ibid.*
35. *Ibid.*, Appendix II, pp. 375-81.
36. Mills, *The Ao Nagas*, p. 1.
37. Mills, *The Lotha Nagas*, p. XVIII.
38. *Ibid.*, p. XIX.
39. *Ibid.*
40. *Ibid.*, p. XVIII.
41. Hutton, *The Sema Nagas*, pp. 4-5.
42. *Ibid.*, p. 5.
43. Mills, *The Ao Nagas*, p. 2.
44. *Ibid.*
45. *Ibid.*, Chami; *Ao Nagas*, p. 13.
46. *Ao Nagro*, p. 11.
47. *Ibid.*, p. 8.
48. *Ibid.*, p. 9.
49. *Ibid.*, pp. 9-11.
50. Hutton, *The Sema Nagas*, pp. 6-7.
51. Mills, *The Ao Nagas*, pp. 8-9.
52. *Ibid.*

5

THE NAGA VILLAGE POLITY

The Nagas had diverse forms of self-governing institutions, which may be categorized into the following types[1]:

1. Chieftainship with political power and priestly function concentrated in the same persons as in the case of the Angship of the Konyak Nagas,
2. Chieftainship with political and the economic powers in the hands of the chief as in the case of the Sema chief,
3. Chieftainship with limited powers,
4. Republican type village polity as in the case of Ao Nagas, and
5. Ultra republican village polity as in the case of Angami Naga village polity.

The Chietainship with Political and Religious Functions

The Konyak Naga Chiefs, called *Angs,* used to be not only the chiefs but also the priests of the community. Some of the Angs are very powerful. The Angs of Mon and Chui have many villages with smaller Angs under them. The Angs are advised by their ministers in deciding matters. The ministers are selected by the Ang from various clans of the village.[2] Somewhat similar was the case with Wanchos of Arunachal Pradesh.

The Wancho villages are administered by their chiefs called *Wangham* assisted by the Council of Elders, which is called *Wangchu Wangcha.* Wangchu Wangcha, a well-organized body, not only administers the village, or a group of villages, but is also entrusted with the task of the administration of justice. The Chief is the president of the council. The others include the senior members (who are assigned different responsibilities and are also called ministers), the priest, and the representatives of the various clans. It needs mention that none can become a Wancho chief unless his both the parents have Wangham blood.

The Wancho society has two important sections, namely, the *Wangham,* the chief and the *Wangpen*, the commoner. They believe that this division dates back to the days of the first creation. The chief marries from both the sections and has several wives. The children of the chief from the commoner wife form an intermediate class known as *Wansa*. The children of *Wangsa* form another class called *Wangsu* irrespective of the status of the mother. Wangsu have lower status than that of the Wangsa. Thus, Wancho society has four sections. The post of the Wancho chief goes to the first born son from his Wancha wife (wife with cent-per-cent blood of the chief). In case the chief has no such son, then either his brother's son or the son of the chief of the parental village succeeds him.[3]

Chieftainship with Political and Economic Power Concentrated in the Hands of the Chief

The hereditary chieftainship is one aspect of the Sema society, which differentiates it from other Naga tribes. A.W. Davis observes about the same:

> "The chief point in which the Semas differ from the other Naga tribes living in this district is the possession of the hereditary village chiefs. These chiefs have many privileges, *i.e.* their subjects cut their jhums and cultivate them for them for nothing; they get a portion of every animal killed in the chase, and generally are in a position far superior to that of an ordinary Naga headman. These chiefs invariably have three or four wives, and usually large families. It is the custom for the sons as they grow up to start new villages on their own account. We thus find that, as a rule, Sema villages are small as compared with the villages of other Naga tribes."[4]

Hutton has written about the succession of chieftainship among the Semas:

> "The chieftainship goes down from father to the son, the elder

sons becoming chiefs in their own villages during the father's lifetime, provided the sons are able to found separate villages, and one of the younger sons probably succeeding in his father's village. Where, however, the elder sons are not able to found villages of their own, the eldest son succeeds his father and his brothers become sort of satellites. In some cases, of course, the chief is succeeded by his brother, on his death, however, the office reverts to the elder line."[5]

The land in Sema villages get divided and sub-divided among the brothers if they are unable to throw out colonies. However, the unmarried younger brothers do not necessarily get share if the father dies. Like the land, the right to free labour is also apt to split where the chief's sons cannot separate. As the subjects owe the chief various services, the former cannot leave the village without the consent of the latter. The chief, however, looks after his subjects, provides them with wives, often feeds them or lends them food in times of scarcity.[6]

The Chang Nagas have also their chiefs in every village. The founder of the village becomes the chief of that village. He is called *Sangbushou*. The chieftainship is hereditary in his family.[7] But, they are not as powerful as the Sema chiefs, as they do not have the same monopoly of land as the latter have.[8]

The chief (*Lowang*) and the council of elders (called *ngongthun* or *ngothun* or *ngothit*) are responsible for the administration and the administration of justice among the Nocte Nagas.The village council's chairman is the chief. Others in the council include *Ngongba* (priest and the minister), *Ramba* (priest and the one who informs the village about any activity), *Noktang* or *Kampa* (six elderly persons from various clans), and now-a-days, the *gaonbura* nominated by the government. Tangsa Nagas of Arunachal Pradesh used to have their very powerful elected chiefs, called *Lungwang* (also called *Lowang* or *Ngowa*). He was assisted by the council of elders elected by the villagers. The elected elders were called *Sangta* or *dedwa* or *kamba*. Many Tangsa sub-tribes or even the villages used to have their respective councils of elders with different nomenclature for the council, etc. There were other differences also from one sub-tribe to another. Usually, the chief was elected from a particular clan and elders from various other clans.[9]

The Zemi Nagas are ruled over by *Kadepeo.* The priest, called *Gekungme,* was the next influential and powerful person in the village. The Kadepeo and the village council had the power to banish a person from the village for committing serious crime or for disobeying their verdict. Kabuis or Roungmeis have *Khumbu,* who is the founder of the village or his descendant. He is the nominal and powerless hereditary chief of the village. *Khulakpa,* chosen by a body of the village elders, called *Thoupei,* exercises real power. Once elected, he may continue life-long on that post and his son may even succeed him subject to the approval of the *Thoupei.* Thoupei is the administrative body of the village. It also administers justice.[10]

Tangkhul society consisted of the chieftains and the commoners. The headman of the village used to be the head of the panchayat (*Hangnga*) consisting of the clan representatives. The administration of justice according to their customary law was done by the panchayat. However, the verdict of the headman used to be final and binding. The person, who used to seek signs and omens was considered to be number one among the chieftains. He was responsible for the security of the village and his consent was essential for declaration of war. In his absence, the number one warrior of the village did his duties, and if desired by the headman, he was allowed to seek signs and omens also. The Tangkhul villages also had the officers with the Manipuri titles of *Khullakpa* and *Lulakpa.* The Tangkhuls also had a higher organization, called *'Long'* with headmen as its members. Its chairman is called *'Longva'.* It is purely a communal organization of the Tangkhul Nagas after the advent of the administration.[11] The Mao Naga village affairs are run by the headman (*Mohou*) and the council of elders selected from every clan according to their customary laws. The administration of justice is done by the council of elders. The chief has all the powers related to 'Mani' or 'genna' days.[12]

Rublican Type

The Ao Nagas have the Council of Elders called Tatars, elected from every clan of the village. The village councils are responsible for the administration of justice, and now-a-days, even for the development activities of the village.[13] Each Ao village is a small republic. A.W. Davis has written: "Each village amongst the Aos is a small republic and each man is as good as his neighbour, indeed it would be hard to find anywhere else more thoroughly democratic communities."[14]

Ultra-republican Village Polity

The Angami Nagas have neither the village chiefs, nor the dully elected village councils. The Angami villages are found to have internal cohesion and they do not lack internal discipline in spite of the lack of chieftainship and the village councils. The whole village gathers in case of any dispute; anybody who has to say something is heard, and after hours of prolonged and tiring discussions, they arrive at certain decision or consensus, and the dispute is settled.[15]

Hutton has beautifully summed up the village polity scenario of the Nagas in the following words:

> "Turning to the polity of the village, different tribes have very different customs. Among the Semas a system of hereditary chiefs exists, each chief having an almost feudal position as the lord of the manor of his village, a system which seems to have obtained among the Kacharis, as the remnants of it are still perceptible among the remote Kachari villages of the south-west of the Naga Hills. The Changs have a system of chiefs very like that of the Semas, and both may be compared in this respect to the Thado Kukis, though among the latter the system is more elaborately developed. The Konyaks too have hereditary chiefs in the Thendu section of the tribe, though not in the Thenkoh division, but among the Konyaks the priestly side of the chieftainship seems more prominent than among other Naga tribes chiefs. On the other hand, the Ao and Tangkhul villages are governed by bodies of elders representing the principal kindreds in the village, while the Angami, Rengma and Lotha and apparently Sangtam villages are run on lines of democracy, a democracy so extreme in the case of the Angami that, in view of his peculiar independence of character, it is difficult to comprehend how his village held together at all before they were subject to the British Government. The Angami has, however, hereditary priests, office descending in the line of the first founder of the village in question."[16]

The founders of the villages and their descendants had very little power among the Angamis. The Lothas had comparatively peaceful state of affairs as, unlike Semas and Angamis, they did nor suffer due to paucity of land. Each village was ruled by a chief (*ekyung*) assisted by an informal council of elders during the days when wars were more frequent. The chieftainship was hereditary in the family of the founder of the village. However, it did not necessarily pass from father to the son. The chief was mainly the war leader among the Lothas and the end of war due to Pax Britanica put an end to his role. Thus the post of *ekyung* virtually ceased to be. The affairs of the Lotha villages were managed after that by the informal council of old and influencial men and the headmen selected by the government. The old men inflicted fines of pork in petty cases and eat the fine and therefore were called *satsoi* (meat-eaters).[17] It may be mentioned that the Ao councillors also eat a fine of pork.[18]

The land in the Naga society belonged to the clans, chiefs[19] and the individuals. The village council, or the chief as the case may be, allotted the land for cultivation to the individuals for jhum period. Such things were not needed in the case of terraced cultivation.

REFERENCES

1. B.B. Kumar, *Introduction to the Naga Tribes,* Meerut, Pragati Prakashan (1997), p. 53.
2. Hokishe Sema, *Emergence of Nagaland,* p. 167.
3. Srivastava, L.R.N., *Among the Wanchs;* Shillong (1970), p. 4.
4. A.W. Davis, in *Census of India,* 1891, Assam, Vol. I, p. 226.; cited in *The Nagas in the Nineteenth Century,* p. 372.
5. J.H. Hutton, *The Angami Nagas,* p. 358.
6. *Ibid.*
7. B.B. Kumar, *Society and Culture in a Corner of Nagaland.*
8. Hutton, *op. cit.,* p. 379.
9. B.B. Kumar, *Introduction to the Nagas,* pp. 55-56.
10. *Ibid.,* p. 54.
11. B.B. Kumar, *Introduction to the Nagas,* p. 63.
12. *Ibid.,* p. 65.
13. *Ibid.,* p. 56.
14. A.W. Davis, *Census of India,* 1891, Assam.
15. Kumar, *op. cit.,* p. 57.
16. Hutton, *Introduction of The Lotha Nagas* by J.P. Mills, p. xxxiii.
17. J.P. Mills, *The Lotha Nagas.,* p. 96.
18. J.P. Mills, *The Ao Nagas,* p. 194.
19. Hokishe Sema, *op. cit.,* pp. 168-69.

6

THE NAGA LANGUAGES

There is more linguistic diversity in the Naga inhabited area than anywhere in the country. The Nagas speak more than three dozen languages and dialects. These languages are mutually unintelligible with diverse linkages. The Naga languages are differently classified by different scholars.

Grierson's Classification

Grierson was the first to conduct a massive study of the Indian languages in his *Linguistic Survey of India* and to classify them. He placed Naga languages under the Assam-Burmese Branch of the Tibeto-Burman languages. Grierson classified the Naga languages into following three groups[1]:

1. Western Naga group: It includes Angami (Tenyidie), Chokri, Kheza, Sema and Rengma.
2. Central Naga group of languages include Ao, Lotha, Sangtam and Yimchungru.
3. Eastern Naga group of languages has Konyak and Chang languages.

Dr. Grierson in his Report also places many Naga languages between the Naga and Bodo, as well as Naga and Kuki group of languages. There is a group of languages between Angami Naga and the Bodo languages, which he called the Naga-Bodo group, bridging over the difference between the characteristic features of the two forms of speech, and similarly between Angami Naga and the Kuki languages there is another group, which he called the Naga-Kuki.

The Naga-Bodo group consists of two main languages, viz., Mikir and Kachcha Naga. Subordinate languages, closely akin to but not dialects of, Kachcha Naga, are Kabui Naga and Khoirao Naga. As might be expected, the Bodo language with which they show the most important points of kinship is the eastern one—Chutiya; while Angami and Lotha are the two Naga tongues to which they are most closely allied. It must, however, be confessed that in regard to Kabui and Khoirao the classification is somewhat arbitrary, for, though they have undoubted connection with the Bodo languages, they also show many points of contact with the Kuki ones. Sir Charles Lyall has given good reasons for declining to accept the inclusion of Mikir in this group and finds evidence for grouping it with the Kuki-Chin languages.[2]

The Naga-Kuki sub-group includes Sopvoma or Mao Naga, Maram, Miyangchang, Kwoireng or Liyang, Luhupa or Luppa language, *viz.,* Tangkhul and Maring. The language of the Mao Nagas most nearly approaches the true Naga language. Of these it possesses the closest resemblance to Kezhama. Indeed, Sopvoma is so closely connected with all the languages of the Western sub-group (in which are included Angami, Sema, Rengma and Kezhama), that it might with equal propriety be classed as belonging to it as to the Naga-Kuki one. The three languages—Sopvoma, Tangkhul and Maring—exhibit a regular gradation in the change of speech. Among them, Sopvoma/Mao is most nearly connected with the Western Naga languages, and Maring with the Kuki ones, while Tangkhul occupies an intermediate position. The Chirus speak a language, which belongs to the old Kuki sub-group of the Kuki-Chin languages, in which its fellows are Rangkhol, Bete, Hallam, Langrong, Aimol, Kolrhen, Kom, Cha, Hmar, Anal, Hiroi-Lamgang and Purum. This last must not be confused with the Naga village of the same name, which belongs to the Maram group.[3]

There are languages connected with typical Naga dialects, with Kuki elements, the influence of which gradually diminishes as we recede from the area occupied by Kuki tribes. We have languages related in part to Bodo dialects, in part to Naga languages, while containing Kuki elements. It is clear that we have in this area a rich variety of dialects due to the effect of the confluence of two, if not of three, streams of languages. And in regard to custom the same hold true. The more detailed our examination, the more would it be possible to augment our display of variety, and to emphasise the remarkable graduation and series of development.[4]

Linguistic Phylum Concept

Grierson's classification of the languages were found to be unsatisfactory after more materials on Tibeto-Burman languages were collected and studied. It led to Linguistic Phylum Concept. A linguistic Phylum is the macro family of languages and the Tibeto-Burman linguistic Phylum consists of nine language families, five of which are found in India, which are: (*a*) Tibetan, (*b*) Kam-Tai, (*c*) r-Gyarung-Mishmi, (*d*) Bodo-Tangsa-Kachin, and (*e*) Kuki-Naga family of languages. Thus, Tangsa and other Naga languages belong to different language families according to this classification.[5]

Benedict's Classification

The *Sino-Tibetan Conspectus* by Paul K. Benedict was published by Cambridge University Press in 1972. It provided an entirely new scheme for the classification of the Sino-Tibetan languages. Six out of the seven group of the languages proposed by Benedict are found in India. According to their scheme of classification, Konyak may be included in the Bodo-Garo or Barish group of languages. Kuki-Naga languages include Mikir, Meithei and Mru. Benedict's study is important from phonological and syntactical view-point. This classification is also not fool-proof as (*i*) it goes with multiple 'perhapses', and (*ii*) the study of the lexeme shall prove that there are multiple cross-correspondences, which often defy geographical and classificatory classifications.[6]

Later Classifications

Bibliography of Sino-Tibetan Languages by R. Shafer in two volumes was published from Wiebaden in 1957 and 1964. He includes the Naga Languages of Manipur and some languages of southern Nagaland in the Kuki language group. G.E. Marrison, in his '*The Classification of the Naga Languages of the North East India* (unpublished Ph.D. dissertation, two volumes, London, 1967) finds the close relationship of the Naga languages with the literary Tibetan, since the modern spoken dialect of Lhasa has developed characteristics, which do not always have close parallel in the Naga languages. Shafer also claims that the phonemes of Burmese and that of certain Naga languages show regular correspondence, which is more true of the written Burmese than the spoken Burmese. His classification of the Naga languages is based on typological comparison at the phonological, morphological and syntactical levels. The phonological sequences are subdivided into syllabic patterns as occurring in the word initial, word-medial and word-final. Morrison arranges Naga languages—from North-East to South-West—into three groups, namely A, B and C groups which are further divided into different types, which are given below[7]:

1. Type A. 1 consists of Tangsa (Yogli), Tangsa (Moshang), Nocte and Wancho languages.
2. Type A. 2 consists of Konyak, Phom and Chang languages.
3. Type B. 1 consists of Tangsa (Yacham), Ao (Chongli and Mongsen) and Sangtam languages.
4. Type B. 2 has Lotha, Yimchungru, Ntenyi and Meluri languages.
5. Type B. 3 consists of Tangkhul and Maring languages.
6. Type C.1 consists of Sema, Angami (Kohima and Khonoma dialects), Chokri, Kheza and Mao languages.
7. Type C. 2 consists of Rengma, Maram, Khoirao/Nzieme, Zeme, Liangmei, Puiron and Nruanghmei.

In phonology, the two types of group A does not differ much except that /r/ does not occur in Type A.2. Type A.1 has somewhat greater accession of items from Kachin and Thai vocabulary. Type B.1 languages have relatively simple phonological system, slightly modified from common Naga form. Type B. 2 is a mixed one with dominant element akin to Ao and the minor part having Southern affiliation. Type B. 3 languages are also linguistically mixed, have important affinities with Ao, which is geographically relatively remote, and have also the elements of the Nruanghmei type with possible borrowings from Manipuri and Kuki languages of the South.[8]

Languages of Type C. 1, with certain amount of specialized vocabulary, have distinctive phonology including voiceless liquids and nasals; and except the Sema language, these languages have initial clusters of which their second cluster is /r/. Normally, these languages do not use consonantal finals. The languages of Type C. 2 extensively use pre-nasalized consonants together with prefixes, such as a- he- ka- ca- in the various languages, which provide an extensive system of morphological prefixation. These languages have many lexical affinities with Angami and other languages of Type C. 1. However, the cognative words in the two groups are highly contrasted at the phonological level.[9]

According to Morrison, only certain languages show close similarity from one to another at all levels, while exhibiting significant differences from the rest at the same time at least at some level. The languages showing difference are less easy to group and they exhibit mixed or transitional features. The six sub-groups whose members show a close similarity at all levels are the following.[10]

(*i*) Angami (Khonoma), Angami (Kohima), Chokri, Kheza, and Mao.

(*ii*) Ao (Chongli), Ao (Mongsen) and Yacham Tangsa.

(*iii*) Chang, Konyak and Phom.

(*iv*) Liangmei and Nruanghmei (Rongmei).

(*v*) Nzieme and Zeme.

(*vi*) Nocte, Tangsa (Moshang), Tangsa (Yogli) and Wancho.

The consonants occurring at the word-initial in different levels in the Naga languages[11] are given below.

Reconstructed common Tibeto-Burman

p	t	c	k
p^h	t^h	c^h	k^h
b	d	j	g
m	n	n	n
	s		h
	r		
	l		
w		y	

Angami (Type C.1)

			Initials
p	t	c	k
p^h	t^h	c^h	k^h
b	d	j	g
m	n	n	n
m^h	n^h	n^h	
f	s		
v	z		h
	r		
	r^h		
	l		
	l^h		
w		y	
wh			

Ao groups (Type B. 1)

p	t	c	k
b	d	j	g
m	n	n	n
	s	š	
	z		
	r		
	l		
w		y	

Konyak group (Type A. 2)

p	t	c	k
p^h	t^h	c^h	k^h
b	d	j	g
m	n	n	n
	s	$š^h$	
	l		
w		y	

It may be mentioned that Morrison arranged them according to the Indian phonetic system, (like 'k, kh, g, gh, n)[12].

General Characteristics

Some of the general characteristics of the Languages of the Nagas[13], though not shared by all, are given hereafter.

Phonetic Charracteristics

(*i*) These languages usually do not use aspirated voiced stops.

(*ii*) A tendency of converting unaspirated voiceless stop into aspirated voiceless stop is visible in many languages. The conversion continues in many cases, leading to /h/ and finally into /y/. In some languages, the distinction betweeen unaspirated voiceless stops and aspirated voiced stops is not clear. An Ao often pronounces 'book' as 'puk'.

(*iii*) Frequent interchangeability between surds and sonants, as well as between /r/ and /l/; and some times between /l/ and /n/ is also the peculiarity of other Indian languages.

(*iv*) Some languages are tonal and the same word pronounced in different tones has different meaning. The Angami language is highly tonal and is musical to hear.

Morphological/Syntactical

(*i*) These languages find difficulty in forming words with abstract ideas/abstract nouns.

(*ii*) The words, in many cases, are found to have interchangeable roles as noun, verb and adjective.

(*iii*) The languages are agglutinative in nature showing varying degree of inflections. Usually expressed by affixes without changing the roots. But they show monosyllabism and isolating structure in lesser degree.

(*iv*) They exhibit pronominal agreement expressed without verb affixual structure.

(*v*) Modifying words and particles expressing voice, mode, direction, aspect, etc. usually precedes the nouns and verbs.

(*vi*) Some languages use generic particles with numerals; these languages usually suffix multipliers to form higher numerals.

(*vii*) Usually, the languages lack grammatical gender; numerals are often inferred by context. Most of the languages lack proper declension.

Wider Linkages

Naga languages, like all other Indian languages follow 'SOV' (subject object verb) syntactical pattern. Only Kashmiri and Khasi, among Indian languages, follow 'SVO' pattern in their sentences. Most of the characteristics given above are not the exclusive characteristics of the Naga languages, but are shared by a large number of Tibeto-Burman, and some even by non-Tibeto-Burman, languages.

Although, there have been many attempts to classify the Naga languages, none of them has been satisfactory. In many cases, the languages, separated geographically, culturally and otherwise from them are found to have many similarities. The lexical similarity between the Ao, a member of the Central Naga group of languages which shows maximum similarity with the Tibetan, and the Meithei, expected to be nearer to the Burmese, is revealing[14]:

Ao	Manipuri	English
Mi	Mei	fire
Ki (House)	ka (room)	–
Yi	You	Wine
Kut	Khut	hand
Ita	Tha	moon/month
Long	Nung	stone
Auja	Nga	fish
Ana	Ani/Ane	two
Asem	Ahum	Three
Trek	Taruk	Six

Here it needs mention that the lexical linkages of the Naga languages are not restricted to the languages of the Tibeto-Burman family alone. The Nagas have received ethnic elements from far and wide, and therefore, the linguistic elements also. The following quote from a discussion in the Anthropological Institute make my point clear:

> "Mr. Hyde Clarke, in responding to Col. Godwin-Austin's observations as to the diversity of languages, proposed another explanation. Thus for monkey there were four words, for *elephant* three. That these were not of local origin could be proved by tracing their affinities elsewhere, and then we find the four forms for monkey, *takwi, simai, veh,* and *suchi,* represented as *tekawu, dsima, wai,* and *tsakar;* the forms for elephant, *lokniu, puok,* and *shiti,* appearing as *ulonga, opowo,* and *ndshogo.* So in like way for many other words, as tiger, cow, goat, fish, head, ear, hair, mouth, hand, bone, blood, sun, moon, star, day, night, to-day, to-morrow, no, not, I, we, thou, you, he, they. Indeed, wherever tested, the general results were the same. Not only was this found to be so as to dissimilar roots, but as to dialectic variations for the ma and nak of not, for the masi and nasi of cow. These facts serve to show the position of the naga languages, and to throw light on the early Naga history. The languages must be those of tribes, forming a league before the occupation of the Naga country, and becoming diversified or distinguished after occupation, not being variants from one original stock. Another result is this, that languages belong to much higher culture than that now prevailing among the Nagas, and to a very ancient culture. The relation is to the group which included the Akkad, the Khita, and all that the speaker had described as Khitoid. One curious parallel in this way is with the Eten or Eteng of Peru, a similar isolated population. The languages are not those of population in the present condition of the Nagas, but of higher populations and apparently of a white race."[15]

He further said:

"The Nagas represent sections of populations governed by a former dominant race driven up into the mountains, and there is no reason to assume that the Nagas are descendants of the dominant race, or that they have not been affected by the intermarriage or immigration of the neighbouring races. They transmit in all probability the languages of the races which gave the earliest culture to India, antecedent to the Kolarians and the Dravidians. There is not much difficulty in fixing this, as the ancient river and town names of India preserved by the classic geographers conform to those found in other parts of Asia and in Europe, occupied by corresponding dominant populations, and which names are consequently anterior to the Aryans. The Naga languages are invaluable for investigations in pre-historic philology and archaeology, and in this sense the tables of Colonel Woodthorpe are of more than local importance."[16]

Pan-Indian Linguistic Characteristics

Many Naga languages use score system of counting. As for example, for Chang Nagas, 'hundred' is 'five scores' and 'one hundred and forty' is 'seven scores'. Dual use of first person plural (exclusive and inclusive) is also not uncommon. These traits are generally shown by a large number of Indian languages and mostly by the Munda languages. Moreover, the Naga languages also use glutteral stops. These traits, which are not the characteristics of the Tibeto-Burman languages, link Naga languages with other Indian languages.[17]

Intra-Tribe Dialectical Variations

The Naga tribes not only have the inter-tribe diversity; but they have also the intra-tribe diversity in the case of their languages. In many cases, the languages differ only phonetically. But there are cases, where the differences are real. Some tribes speak different languages in different villages. There are examples where the same woman speaks to her husband and the son in different languages.[18]

Script

The Naga languages were only spoken languages which did not have any script of their own. Christian Missionaries started the use of the Roman script in the latter part of the nineteenth century for writing their languages, in which they translated Bible tracts and latter on even the whole Bible. Dr. E.W. Clark, the first Baptist Missionary in Nagaland, wrote the *Ao Naga Dictionary*. His wife prepared *Ao Naga Grammar*. R.B. McCabe wrote *Outline Grammar of the Angami Language*. Dr. W.G. Witter of the American Foreign

Mission Society wrote *Outline Grammar of the Lotha Naga Language*. These publications used Roman script. The textbooks in various Naga languages are also published by the Government of Nagaland in which Roman script is used.

The Christian Missionaries selected particular dialect from each of the Naga languages for the translation of the Bible. The dialect so selected in long run became the standard literary language of that tribe. As for example, the Chongli dialect of the Aos, in which Bible was translated, is their literary language today.

The Nagaland Bhasha Parishad, Kohima, a voluntary organization, has published lexicon of 64 tribal languages, grammars and self-teachers of about one and half a dozen of them and folklore of some tribal languages. The publications used Devanagari script. Devanagari and Roman scripts have been used for the languages of Nagaland.

The Nagas have a legend according to which they also had their script.

Nagamese/Naga Pidgin

Nagamese is a pidgin developed by the Nagas. Its grammar is the simplified form of Assamese grammar. The lexeme was mostly taken from the Assamese, Hindi and Nepali. It follows the phonetic pattern of different sub-groups of the Naga languages. The origin and growth of Nagamese is the index of the close relationship of the hills and plains in the North-East region. It was mostly necessitated due to the needs of the multi-glot Nagas for interaction with its neighbours

The Linguistic Diversity and the Myth of Isolation

It is usually found that mutually unintelligible languages do not have entirely distinct vocabulary. It is true in the case of the Naga languages also. A few sets of lexemes may make difference due to permutation and the combination. Again a known word may become unintelligible due to phonetic change or if prefix, suffix or infix is added. In Nagaland, different sections of the same tribe are found to use different words for mother. They represent different waves of the people forming the tribe. This phenomena was possible only if the people could freely move and live together. Again to affect the permutation and combination of three or four sets of lexemes to form, say three dozen languages, presupposes the co-existance and living together of the people speaking diverse languages. The steps may be living together, becoming bilingual, pidgin formation and random de-lexification or droping of a set of the lexeme. Such explanation is not possible if we accept the myth of isolation.

Conclusion

The diversity of the Naga languages is the indicator of their ethnic diversity by way of incorporation of human elements from diverse sources besides interactions with neighbouring societies and cultures.

REFERENCES

1. Grierson, George Abraham, *Linguistic Survey of India*, Vol. III, Part II.
2. Lyall, *The Mikirs*, pp. 152-72.
3. Grierson, *op. cit.*
4. *Ibid.*
5. Kumar, Dr. B.B., *Tribal Languages and Literature*, in *The Tribal Societies of India*, p. 106.
6. *Ibid.*, p. 107.
7. Shreedhar, M.V., *Naga Pidgin: A Sociolinguistic Study of Inter-Lingual Communication Pattern in Nagaland*, pp. 29-30.
8. *Ibid.*, p. 30.
9. *Ibid.*, pp. 30-31.
10. *Ibid.*, p. 31.
11. *Ibid.*, pp. 32-33.
12. *Ibid.*, p. 31 n.1.
13. Kumar, *op. cit.*, pp. 205-06.
14. *Ibid.*, pp. 206-07.
15. *Journal of the Anthropological Institute*, Vol. XI, pp. 52-73 and pp. 196-214; cited in Elwin's *Nagas in the Nineteenth Century*, pp. 82-83.
16. *Ibid.*, p. 83.
17. See B.B. Kumar's paper in the *Highlander*, Vol. 1, No. 1; also see *Outline Grammars of various Naga Languages* by B.B. Kumar, published by Nagaland Bhasha Parishad, Kohima.
18. Mills in his *The Ao Nagas* (p. 3) has written about Sangratsu, an Ao village: "of the two *"khels"* of Sangratsu one consists of Mongsen clans speaking the Mongsen dialect, and other of Chongli clans speaking the Chongli dialect—the two not twenty yards apart. Each *"khel"* knows the other's language but speaks its own, and a Mongsen woman married to a man of the Chongli *"khel"* will speak Mongsen to her husband but Chongli to her baby, for the child is Chongli like his father and must be brought up to speak Chongli."

7

MORUNG INSTITUTION AMONG THE NAGAS

The youth dormitories, under many forms and names, existed in a very wide region of the world extending from the Himalayas and the Formosa in the North to the Australia and New Zealand on the South; and from the eastern Pacific and Marquesas to the west coast of Africa. Thus this social institution is found among diverse races, now classed as distinct, such as Dravidians, Indo-Mongols, Malays, Papuans, Polynesians, Australians and Africans. As Peal observes: "Taken by themselves, these barracks for the unmarried are sufficiently suggestive; but when we notice that they are but one of many peculiar social customs found surviving more or less among all these races, the case is doubly noteworthy, first as evidence of former racial affinity; second as an important factor in social evaluation generally.[1]

The institution of bachelors' dormitory or Men's House is found among a large number of tribes in India, such as, *Ghotul*[2] of Murias, *Dhumkuria*[3] of Oraons, *Nedrong*[4] of Dimasa Kacharis, *Maro* or *Terang*[5] of Mikirs, *Moshup*[6] of Adis and *Morungs*[7] of the Naga tribes. The word 'Morung', commonly used in the North-East India, in not a tribal language word. It is the word of the Ahom language.[8] Different tribal languages have different words for it.[9]

The youth dormitories do not follow uniform pattern. All the tribes do not have it. There are cases where boys and girls use the same dormintory. Asurs, Marias and some other Gond tribes and Khonds have common dormitories where young boys and girls sleep together. Oraons, Mundas, Adis, Sherdukpens, Zemi Nagas, Chang

Nagas and Gonds of Chanda have separate dormitories for boys and girls. Birhors, Birijias, Karbis, Dimasa Kacharis, Garos, Maghs, Mizos, Koms, Vaipheis, Paites, Kabui Nagas, Angami Nagas (*Kichuki*), Lotha Nagas (*Champo*), Rengma Nagas (*Rensi/Azughu*; *Awikhu* of the eastern Rengmas), Ao Nagas (*Arichu*), Konyak, Wangcho, and Phom Nagas have only the Young Men's dormitories. Morung was practically non-existant or found in miniature form only among the Sema Nagas. Their Young bachelors used to sleep in chief's house on pounding tables. The institution did not exist among Sauria Pahariyas, Gonds of Mandla, Chhindwara, Betul and Balaghat, and among many other tribes.[10]

The institution also imparted sex-education where young boys and girls had common dormitories. The entry of women was strictly prohibited in the morungs of the Lothas, Aos and the Rengmas. Angami Morung (*Kichuki*) was used only as a casual resort. The boys did not sleep there. It was also used on certain occasions like Thezukepu genna.[11] As observed by Hutton, among the Angamis, "The morung is not habitually used by the young men as it is in the Aos and trans-Dikhu tribes, but it is used on the occasion of the ceremonies and gennas which by traditional use call for a house definitely allowed to the young men of the clan."[12] Thus morung was an insignificant institution with the Angamis and might have been decayed among the Semas.[13] As observed by Hutton, "As a general rule", among the Semas, "the Chief's house serves all the purposes of the morung, both as a centre of gennas and as bachelors' sleeping place."[14]

The boys among the Ao, Rengma and the Lotha Nagas were admitted to their morungs on attainment of certain age where they slept at night for a definite period of time or till married.[15] Morung among the Chang Nagas, called *Haki* in their languages, is not a bachelors' dormitory. They have separate boys' and girls' dormitories, called '*sochem*' and '*shemshimang*' respectively. The Changs also have separate sitting and meeting platforms called '*puhshin*' in every *khel* (section of the village).[16] These four social institutions of the Chang Nagas need discussion in detail due to their highly differentiated functions.

Scholars have expressed different views about the origin and purpose of the morungs. According to Hudson, it would seem to be rather symptomatic of a definite level of culture than distinctive of any special ethnic group or groups.[17] Morung possibly "is a survival of the communal house form which private dwellings split off" is the opinion of Peal.[18] "The object of the dormitory was to prevent incest" was the observation of Shakespeare.[19] Elwin was of the view that "It was instituted to save children from witnessing the primal scene", and "from being an embarrassment to their parents."[20] Morung according to Elwin, was the guard-room of the Nagas.[21] Haimendorf was of the view that: "The Morung belongs together with the log drum, the oldest cultural stratum of the Naga Hills."[22]

Morungs played vital role in the social, educational, cultural and religious life of the Nagas. Anand observes:

> "The morung plays vital role in preparing younger generations for posts in the village council. The morung is the club, the public school, the military training centre, the hostel for boys and meeting place for village elders. It is as well the centre for the social, religious and political activities. In short, it is the fulcrum of the village democracies."[23]

In spite of the great role played by this institution, it never interfered or encroached the economic and social functions of the family. The observation of Haimendorf about the institution is quoted below:

> "Nowhere in the Naga Hills—can the men's house be considered as replacing a boy's parental home. Its function is altogether different: by entering the morung a boy gains admission to the society of men, without, however, severing his ties with his own family. Throughout life for the unmarried son, for the young married man, who perhaps at the height of his importance in morung affairs sets up a household of his own, as well as for the seasoned village elders—institution of some Naga tribes, absorbs much of the men's social and political energies, there is no conflict between a man's loyalty to his morung and his obligations towards his family household. Family and morung satisfy different social needs and are in no way mutually exclusive."[24]

Morungs used to be the centre of social education. But the

institution did not play uniform role. The young ones of Lohra, Chik Baraik, etc. did not join village dormitories, as they received education of their respective crafts from their parents. These craft practising communities are interspersed among other tribes of Eastern/Central India. The defence role of the morungs was more prominent among many Naga tribes. Among Dimasa Kacharis, the morungs did not have roofs precisely due to reasons of defence. In many tribes, the morung's location near the village gate also points towards the same.

The morungs, among the Central and Eastern Nagas and Xylophones or log drums to announce the arrival of the enemy or of any eminent danger, were importanr part of their culture. Log-drum was the most important feature of the Chang Haki. It was placed in the middle of the Haki covering the plinth area by length. It was hollowed trunk of a tree with carved buffalo head on one end and the tail on the other. The Aos had also similar log-drums.[25] It needs mention that buffalo horns were also carved on the house posts of the Chang Nagas as a sign of wealth.[26] It is interesting to note that Hutton has associated buffalo with Mon-Khmer culture and mithun with Tibeto-Burman culture. It may be erroneous, however, to derive any conclusion on this fact, keeping in view the nixed culture of the Nagas. Moreover, Changs used to sacrifice both buffalo and mithun in their religious rites. Buffalo, a swamping creature is reared by non-rice producing Changs but not by the rice-producing terraced cultivator Angamis.[27] The drums point towards intra-tribal differences among the Nagas, as well as inter-tribal linkages with non-Naga tribes. Northern Sangtams, Aos, Konyaks, Yimchungrus and Changs "make enormous drums out of a whole tree hollowed through a narrow slit in the top ... But the Southern Nagas—Lothas, Semas, South Sangtams, Rengmas, Angamis etc. do not make these drums at all."[28] However, the Wa of Burma make drums of this sort.[29] Unlike the drums of the Changs, mentioned above, the ends of the drums of Aos, Konyaks and Northern Sangtams are "carved usually with a mithun head and hornbill tail respectively."[30] The wooden drum, *sheku,* made out of huge hollowed tree, is not a genuine Sema instrument. It is only found in the village containing appreciable admixture of Sangtam blood.[31] It is beaten for deaths, wars and various gennas. It is not used, however, at death ceremony among the

Aos. Unlike Konyaks and Changs, they use hide drums on such occasions.[32]

Xylophone's association with morung is well-known.[33] Its making, consecration and use is associated with certain rules and rituals.[34] The suggested connection of the log-drum with canoes, points towards the Naga links with the Austranasians.[35]

The construction of the morung was the prerequisite for the establishment of a new village. Different sections (*khels*) of the villages used to have their respective morungs: some had more. Morungs assumed special prominence during Moatsu festival of the Aos.[36] Heads of the victims, the human effigies and skulls of the sacrificial victims were hung in the morungs.[37] Presents to the head-takers were given there.[38] Sacrificial mithun was brought to the morung before purchase.[39] Morung was repaired as rain charm.[40] The Semas used to build miniature morungs as fertility rite.[41] Strict discipline was maintained in the morung and one was even fined for the gossips therein.[42] Among Changs, the man under genna used to stay in the morung.[43] Lothas used to keep sacred stones there.[44] It was also used by the bridegroom[45] among the Angamis.

Haki/Morungs of the Chang Nagas was a drum house as well as repository of the trophies of war. It was a guard house of the village during head-hunting days, a council hall and a religious institution. The excellent wood carving art of the Changs (also Phoms) and its singing and dancing got impetus from this institution. Haki of the Changs was not a bachelors' dormitory. Young boys after puberty were given dao-holders as an initiation ceremony. They were allowed to work in the fields after that and sleep in their respective sochem till married.[46] Unmarried Chang girls used to sleep in outer rooms of the house. In reality, they did so in a group and the house used for the purpose was called Shemshimang. Ao Naga girls also used to sleep in a separate house called *Tsuki* (Mills called it *Chiki*) which was chaperoned by a widow.[47] Mundas did the same.[48] Rengmas and Konyaks also had similar girls' dormitories.[49] Konyak Ang girls slept in separate room of the chief's house.[50] Guests were also lodged in morungs of some Naga tribes.

The Changs have a massive platform raised on thick wooden posts about one metre high and a floor covered with plaited bamboo matting and smoothly polished wooden logs serving as benches fixed along three sides of the platform in one side of the village street in every *khel* of the village. It is called *Puhshun*. It is the meeting place for the villagers as well as the sitting place of the village court. It has also the sacrificial stand, known as *qui-qui*; and thus a place for the rituals.

Some points needing mention in the light of the above-mentioned facts is the following:

1. The morung is neither tribe specific, nor geographic nor race specific institution. It is spread over a very wide region of the globe.
2. The functions of the morung vary from tribe to tribe.

REFERENCES

1. Peal, S.E., *The Communal Barracks of Premitive Races*, Science Vol. 20, No. 507 (1982), p. 228.
2. Elein, Verrier, *The Kingdom of the Young: Abridged from the Muria and Their Ghotul;* London Oxford University Press, 1986, p. 23.
3. Roy S.C., *The Oraon of Chota Nagpur*, Ranchi Bar Library, 1915.
4. Danda, Dipali G., *Among the Dimasa of Assam: An Ethnographic Study*, New Delhi, 1978, p. 28.
5. Lyall, Sir Charles, (edit), *The Mikir*, Guwahati, Reprint, p. 11.
6. Roy Sachin, *Aspects of Padam Miniyong Culture*, Shillong, 1966, p. 194.
7. Kumar, Dr. B.B., *The Tribal Societies of India*, 1998, pp. 152-53.
8. *Ibid.*, p. 152.
9. *Ibid.*, pp. 163-68.
10. *Ibid.*
11. *Ibid.*, p. 166.
12. Hutton, *The Angami Nagas*, p. 49.
13. *Ibid.*
14. Hutto, *The Sema Nagas*, p. 37.
15. Mills, J.P., *The Ao Nagas*, pp. 177-78; *The Rengma Nagas*, p. 52; *The Lotha Nagas*, p. 24.
16. Kumar, B.B., *op. cit.*, pp. 158-60.
17. Hodson, T.C., *The Naga Tribes of Manipur,* London, Mcmillan & Co. Ltd., 1911, Reprint, p. 75.
18. Peal, S. E., 'On the Morung' as possibly a Relic of pre-marriage Communism, *Journal of the Anthropological Institute,* Vol. 22 (1893), p. 244.
19. Shakespeare, John, In a foot-note to *The Naga Tribes of Manipur* by T.C. Hodson, p. 86.
20. Elwinn, Verrier, *op. cit.*, p. 23.

21. Kumar, B.B., *op. cit.*, p. 153.
22. Furer Haimendorf, C. Von, The Konyak Nagas, *The Journal of Royal Anthropological Institute*, Vol. 13, pp. 23, 25.
23. Anand, V.K., *Nagaland in Transition*, New Delhi (1967), pp. 91-92.
24. Haimendorf, *Youth Dormitories and Communal Houses in India...*, Anthropos, Vol. 45 (1950), p. 120.
25. Mills, *The Ao Nagas*, p. 77.
26. *Ibid.*, p. 78.
27. Kumar, *Morung Institutions in India*, *op. cit.*, p. 156.
28. Mills, *The Lotha Nagas*, p. XXVIII.
29. *Ibid.*, n. 1.
30. *Ibid.*, p. XXVIII.
31. Hutton, *The Sema Nagas*, p. 52; Kumar, *op. cit.*, pp. 156-59.
32. Mills, *The Ao Nagas*, p. 158.
33. *Ibid.*, p. 79; Kumar, *op. cit.*, p. 158.
34. Mills, *The Ao Nagas*, pp. 78-80, 96, 204, 208, 254, 255, 300., Kumar, *op. cit.*, 156-59.
35. Mills, *The Ao Nagas*, pp. 76 n. l, 79 n. 3, 80 n. 2, 208 n. 1, 227, n. 1.
36. *Ibid.*, pp. 116-17, 119.
37. *Ibid.*, 205-6, 376; Hutton, *The Angami Nagas*, p. 162.
38. Mills, *The Ao Nagas*, p. 186.
39. *Ibid.*, p. 388.
40. *Ibid.*, pp. 131-32.
41. *Ibid.*, p. 208 n. 2.
42. *Ibid.*, pp. 177, 179, 180, 240.
43. Hutton, *The Angami Nagas*, pp. 380-81.
44. *Ibid.*, p. 406.
45. *Ibid.*, pp. 221-23.
46. Kumar, *op. cit.*, pp. 158-59.
47. Mills, *The Ao Nagas*, p. 212.
48. Roy, S.C., *The Mundas and Their Country*, p. 385.
49. Mills, *The Rengma Nagas*, p. 52; Haimendorf, *Konyak Nagas*, p. 27, *Naked Nagas*, p. 96.
50. Haimendorf, *op. cit.*, in S.N. 49.

8

HEAD-HUNTING AMONG THE NAGAS

The Nagas are known as the head-hunters. The practice continued in the Naga Hills district upto the inception of the district in 1866.[1] There were occasional raids in the district by the Nagas of the unadministered Naga areas even after that.[2] The head-hunting continued in unadministered Tuensang upto the dawn of independence and even during 1990. Thus head-hunting is a recent phenomenon for the Nagas. The head-hunting, according to Naga belief, was a fertility rite, which was supposed to bring soul substance, which, in turn, fertilized the soil.[3] Head-hunting provided excellent mechanism of social defence. Every premium was given in taking enemy's head and saving one's own.[4] It was an offensive mechanism of defence generating chain of provocation and revenge.

The head-hunting was not practised only by the Naga tribes. Some Kuki-Chin tribes, such as Thadou Kukis, and the Lakhers also indulged in head-hunting.[5] The Koms, a Kuki-Chin tribe of Manipur, also claim to be head-hunters in the past.[6] Thadous needed a freshly cut head to adore the grave of their chief.[7] Head-hunting is also reported among the tribes of North Borneo.[8] In one form or the other the practice is widespread in various quarters of the globe.[9]

The head-hunter was given maximum honour for successful annihilation of the enemy. At the same time he was subjected to maximum disgrace for losing his own head. The children were not named after a person losing his head and his family suffered many disabilities attached to unnatural death.[10] The Changs used to cut and bring the heads of their own men killed by enemy during expedition in the latter's village[11] so that to avoid their falling in the enemy's hands. In case, a headless body of their clansmen was found, then they used to attach a gourd as head for ceremonial purpose.[12]

The head was the trophy of a successful warrior, which entitled him to special honour and the right to wear the insignia of a head-hunter. The head-hunter was entitled to wear special ornaments and dress.[13] He was specially tattooed among the Konyaks.[14] The decorations on the corpse platform of the head-taker indicated his achievement.[15] He was entitled to special reception by the villagers[16] and received presents from them.[17] The drum beating signified success in head hunting.[18] The number of girls willing to marry a successful head-taker used to increase manyfold. These made the young ones blood-thirsty. The other reasons of war and head-hunting were urge for revenge, anger due to casual or deliberate insult, dispute over land or fishing rights, fishing and hunting in enemy's territory, etc.[19]

The arduous task of bringing the head of the enemy was necessitated to provide proof of the achievement. Hutton writes:

> "Among the Naga tribes, at any rate, head-hunting though associated with a vague idea of the benefits acruing from human sacrifice, must also be connected in no small degree with ordinary everyday human vanity. What man, or at least what Naga, who has killed his enemy does not want to boast about it? And unless he can show the body, where is the proof? Most savages are somewhat economical of truth, at any rate the Naga is when it comes to his exploits in war and the chase. If slayer can produce the body of the slain his statement is likely to be accepted as true, and since retrieving the body would be laborious, not to say, often dangerous proceeding the head is, the natural part of it is bring back as testimony, as it gives a definite assurance that the foe has been killed, not scotched."[20]

The reason given by O. Henry is also worth-quoting:

> "Truely the merry head hunter reduced art and philosophy to a simple code. To take your adversaries head, to basket it at the portal of your Castle, to see it lying there, a dead thing with its cunning and stratagems and power gone—Is there a better way to foil his plots, to refute his arguments, to establish your superiority over his skill and wisdom."[21]

There was an old Lotha custom of vetting any human flesh brought by a warrior during a head-hunting expedition by a board of old men before the head-hunting ceremonies really started.[22] The Chang warriors used to bring even other limbs such as arms, legs and fingers.

The Naga tactics of war included surprise attack and ambush as well as open war. But the latter method of war was rarely resorted to. The challenges were usually sent for open battles against a village, tribe or clan through the mediators of a neutral village to meet at a fixed place and time for open fight. Some warning symbols, such as a sharp bamboo spike or a pod of sharp red-peper, was also usually sent with the messenger to remind them of the smarting consequences. All the able-bodied individuals of both sides participated in such battles. In head-hunting expeditions, in Tuensang, usually the party of raiders with their spears, daos and protective buffalo-hide shields used to march during night with archers on the head of the column and attack the village at day-break when the cock crowed for the second time. They usually slaughtered the unsuspecting inmates coming out of their doors one by one, or otherwise, attacked the village when it was still dark, awaken the villagers by their deafening war cries and by setting the houses on fire, and killed the drowsy villagers running here and there in utter dread and surprise. While returning, they studded the path with sharp bamboo spikes carried in small slender baskets hanging from their belts, just to prevent the pursuers.[23]

Sometimes, the head-hunter used to sneak into the village during day time, while the able-bodied persons of the village were out working in their fields, and cut the head of the women, children or the old. The surprise attacks on the group of persons either going to the field, or during working there or while returning from the field after the work was also not uncommon. The attackers usually encircled the group and massacred all except few who could escape. They usually used to post able-bodied persons to prevent any help coming from the village in response to their cry for help. The woman's head was prized most partly due to the decorative hairs and partly as it needed more valour and feat to get out of the protective cordon of the warriors of enemy camp. There were cases when more than one person speared the victim. In such a case, the first one to spear him claimed and got the head. The others used to divide limbs of the victim among themselves.[24]

The Nagas of Tuensang carried with them during head-hunting expeditions specially stiff, strong and light bags, called Khekyang, made of nettle fibre, and soaked in oil and heated over fire to make it so solid that even water and blood did not pass through the same. They also used it during the game.

The Changs also prepared dangerous snares for killing their enemies. For making smaller one, they used to dig half metre deep pit in a convenient place on an approach path, studded it thickly with sharp bamboo spikes, and covered it with leaves, grass, moss and earth. The unsuspecting victim falling on the same was not killed, but he became lame for the life. About three metres deep ditch was dug usually on a path near a steep slope and studded with two rows of sharp bamboo spikes for preparing second kind of trap. One row of the bamboo spikes were about one and a half metres high, and the other with the lower ones. It was then likewise covered with twigs, moss and earth. The victim, often lured or challenged to run over it considering it to be a part of the path, was speared and killed immediately.[25]

The head-hunting stopped in the Naga Hills district of Assam due to British intervention. But the same continued in Tuensang even after independence. There are many cases when different villages formed a league and attacked a common enemy. This happened after independence during the autumn of 1948 when the Changs of Tobu village mustered the support of twenty villages of the Chang, Phom, Yimchungru and Khiamngan Nagas in their expedition against the powerful Konyak village of Ukha. As per the official report, one thousand Naga warriors participated in the same and 612 Konyaks lost their lives in the war. Ukha, a powerful village situated on the southern tip of the Konyak country, had large number of courageous warriors dreaded by their neighbours. They used to harass their neighbouring villages by assaulting their people, destroying their crops and looting their animals. Other villages hated them, but had no courage to challenge them. One day, Chingmak Chang of the Lower *Khel* of Tobu village went down for fishing in the river between Tobu and Ukha and did not return home. Next day, his headless body was found on the bank of the river. The Changs of

Tobu suspected Ukha men to be the culprits. In wild rage, they swore to avenge the death of their man. It may be pointed out that Tobu is a mixed village with Konyaks and Changs in the Upper and the Lower *Khels* respectively. As mentioned earlier, the village witnessed the bloodiest conflict between the two tribes about four decades after the Ukha battle.

Ukha, as already mentioned, was too powerful to be challenged by the Changs of Tobu alone. They, therefore, sent their prominent persons as emissaries with valuable present of colourful shawls, splendid weapons, cattle, mithuns, etc. to the headmen of the Chang villages and the neighbouring tribes. The emissaries handed over the gifts to them and negotiated terms and conditions for the assistance in the war. Ultimately, they could secure the assurance of help from twenty-seven villages of the region, which included the Chang villages of Hakching, Chingmei and Chentang; Khiamngan villages, Lengnyu, Kengnyu and Nedha, and powerful Pangsha and Panso villages. The following factors facilitate such war alliances:

(*i*) Common enemity for a village among the neighbouring villages;

(*ii*) presents—cattle, mithun, shawl, weapons, etc.—offered as presents to elicit the help from different villages; and

(*iii*) lust for head-hunting and plunder.[26]

It was not for the first time that different villages combined together and formed a league against a common enemy village. Such things happened earlier also, but not at this scale. The raiders from Chang Naga villages of Noksen, Litam, Lungra, Yarr, Champiyatong, Lakstang, Kantak, Langtam and Mozung Jami (Tuensang village) participated in a head-hunting expedition against the Ao Naga villages of Mongsenyimti and Lungkung in as early as January 1888.[27]

The formation of the league of villages generated confidence among the warriors. Otherwise also, the warriors of bigger and aggressive villages were found to be confident of their strength even after the arrival of the British in the Naga inhabited areas. Porteous has described the overweening confidence of the villagers of Tuensang thus:

> "Only overweening confidence in their ability to resist us can account for the policy of the Mojungs in not saving their grain by removal, and only the issue of orders from some common centre can explain the unanimity with which all their villages upto their capital were one after the other devoted to the flames."[28]

The Naga villages fought unitedly against an enemy village. However, it does not mean that there was no internal conflict in a village. Often it was found that different sections of a village (*khels*) were not in good terms with each other, and they had their own defence arrangements. An observation about Tuensang village more than hundred years ago reveals the internal situation of many villages:

> "On examination, the village was found divided into four *khels* (groups) each strongly fortified against its neighbours by a well-pitched ditch. Each *khel* contained about 150 houses, the internal defences indicated a divided community, and divided counsels may partly explain the poor show of resistance made."[29]

Chingmei is a Chang Naga village. Milada Ganguli writes about the internal situation of that village:

> "Unfortunately, the inhabitants of the new village did not live in harmony for long. Disputes broke out over land, occasionally they quarrelled during fishing and hunting expeditions, personal insults too provoked many clashes. As a rule they resulted in violent fighting in which several clansmen lost their lives. Tradition, however, does not permit any one to take the head of a slain inhabitant of the same village."[30]

Head-hunting was prohibited by the British. But the mock head-hunting was practised, as for example among the Lothas, at Rangendri genna (ceremony). The performance of this "genna" did not permit a man to wear any of the ornaments of a warrior, but entitled him to have one representation of a head put on his grave for each time he performed it.[31]

The Nagas also had ceremonies (gennas) attached to the head-hunting. The disposal of the head taken varied from tribe to tribe. Some tribes exposed the head in front of their morungs;[32] the others hung it on the head-tree.[33] The Angamis buried even the head of their enemies.[34]

REFERENCES

1. Bareh, H., *Nagaland District Gazetteer,* Kohima district, p. 63.
2. A large number of the Nagas were massacred in Tobu village of Nagaland in the conflict between the Konyaks and Changs residing there.
3. Bareh, *op. cit.*
4. Kumar, *Tribal Societies of India,* p. 183.
5. Shakespeare, J., *Lushei Kuki Clans,* p. 220.
6. *Ibid.,* p. 155.
7. *Ibid.,* p. 198.
8. Hutton, *The Angami Nagas,* p. 156.
9. *Ibid.,* p. 157.
10. Kumar, B.B., *op. cit.*
11. Mills, J.P., *The Ao Nagas,* p. 225, n. 2.
12. *Ibid.,* p. 229, n. 4.
13. Hutton, *The Angami Nagas,* pp. 29, 30, 32; Mills, *The Ao Nagas,* pp. 37, 41, 42; Mills, *The Lotha Nagas,* pp. 8, 12, 13, 109.
14. Hutton, *op. cit.,* p. 385.
15. Mills, *The Ao Nagas,* p. 281.
16. *Ibid.,* p. 204.
17. *Ibid.,* p. 186.
18. Mills, *The Ao Nagas,* p. 281; Mills, *The Lotha Nagas,* p. 158; Hutton, *The Angami Nagas,* p. 166.
19. Kumar, *op. cit.,* pp. 181-82.
20. Hutton, *op. cit.,* p. 157.
21. *Ibid.,* p. 157, n. 1.
22. *Ibid.,* n. 2.
23. Kumar, *op. cit.,* p. 183.
24. *Ibid.,* pp. 183-84.
25. *Ibid.,* p. 184.
26. *Ibid.,* pp. 186-87.
27. Alemchiba Ao, *Historical Account of Nagaland,* pp. 112-13.
28. *Ibid.,* p. 115.
29. *Ibid.,* pp. 116-17.
30. Ganguli, Milada, *Pilgrimage to the Nagas,* p. 184.
31. Mills, *The Lotha Nagas,* p. 129.
32. *Ibid.,* p. XXIX, n. 2.
33. *Ibid.,* pp. 28, 108, 162 n. 1, 129; heads of the enemies and dummy heads were hung on mingetung (head-tree).
34. *Ibid.,* p. XXXVII.

9

THE NAGA SOCIAL STRUCTURE : STRATIFICATION, DEPRIVATION AND THE COMPLEXITIES

The social structure of the Naga Society was not uniform. It differed from tribe to tribe. There was strict stratification in some cases and egalitarian social structure among some others. Some sections among them were more previleged than the others. Clan-based functional differentiation and the performance of degrading work by certain sections of some tribes were also observed. Acute form of slavery also existed among some Naga tribes. Christianity and modern education has strengthened individualism. Substantial flow of resources from the Central Government has failed to bring desired developmental results. Weakening of the egalitarian ethos continue; the gap between the rich and poor is widening day-by-day.

Social Stratification

The Sema society consists of the Chiefs and the commoners (mughemi; nearest English meaning is 'churl' or 'orphan'). The tie created between the chief and the mughemi is short of mixture of land tenure and adoption. The mughemi is inevitably tied to his chief's village. The chief provides him with land as soon as he marries, and not before, on the understanding that he will do work in his field and will help the chief in war. The son of a chief, accompanied by a number of his father's dependents (mughemi), and also perhaps, by any runaways, thieves, or broken men generally that he can pick up, colonizes new areas; settles new village. When making a new village, where the land taken up is either newly acquired as a result of successful hostilities or has never before been cultivated, he reserves for himself all the land he likes. The remaining land is given to the more prominent companions and the left over to the mughemi whose entire dependence upon himself was beyond question.[1]

The Konyak chiefs or Angs are an exclusive class who take precedence over the other two sections. These chiefs must be of Ang blood by both parents. An Ang chief may have many wives taken from other clans, but his principal wife must be the daughter of an Ang of another village.[2]

The Wancho Nagas have also, somewhat, identical social structure to that of the Konyaks. A Wancho Wangham must have Wangham blood from both parents' side. Apart from the Wangham (chief) and Wangpen (commoner) sections, Wanchos have two more sections—Wangsa and Wangsu—formed due to intermixing of Wangham and Wangpen blood.[3]

The Changs have also chiefs in their villages. However, the Chang chiefs are not as powerful as Sema chiefs, having not the same monopoly of land.[4] Every Western Rengma village used to have chiefs prior to the British occupation of their country. The post was hereditary in the clan but not in the family. In Tseminyu village, the chieftainship was held for many generations in Tepinyu clan after founding of the village. At the end when they began to rule badly then people started deserting the village. There was a revolution and the Khinzonyu clan seized the power. The chief of that clan became cruel and oppressive so that his chieftainship lasted for only seven years. The chieftainship, then passed to the Kentennenyu clan. The chieftainship in that clan lasted for seven generations till the country's annexation by the British. The story is equally interesting in the case of Tesophenyu village. The chieftainship of that village was always held by Khungza clan of lower *khel.* Once Mhatongza clan of upper *khel* made a bid to power; a fierce feud started leading to such fear that none dared to go to the fields leaving their old folk and the property unguarded. Ultimately, to break the deadlock, the wife of the ruling chief suggested a plan, according to which his people started shouting and pretending to go to their fields. The Mhatongza clan believed them and went to their fields. After they went far ahead, the Khungza returned, looted Mhatongza property, burnt their houses, and killed their sentry Kheheche, a runaway from another village and adopted by Mhatongza clan. Thus Mhatongza claim for chieftainship ended; the two clans with a common ancestry, split so completely that they became separate exogamous clans and began to intermarry. The Eastern Rengmas do not remember to have hereditary chieftainship. Disobedience to a chief was punished by the destruction of the house of the offender among the Western Rengmas in the past. The litigation in the courts also weakened the powers of the traditional village authority.[5]

The elements of social stratification is not only restricted to the chieftainship among the Nagas. Even where the democratic functioning of village polity is observed, all the clans do not have equal status. The Aos are controlled nominally by a council of elders (tatars) who deal with disputes in the community and usually exact a fee for dispensing justice. The tribe is divided into two groups—Chongli and Mongsen—speaking practically different languages. Naturally, in majority of Ao villages, one dialect or the other has got the upper hand. Of course, the situation drastically changed once Bible was translated in Chongli dialect and it became the literary language of the Aos. Chongli and Mongsen are again divided into three exogamous clans each. The three exogamous clans (kidong)—Pongen, Langkam and Chami—take precedence in that order and thus have no equal status. The Pongen among them has superior status.[6] The Chang clans—Chongpo (sub-divided into Shangdi, Hangwang, Hagiyung, Ungpong, Maava), Ung, Lumao Kangcho and Kudamji perform different religious functions. Even the personal names differ clan-wise among them.

Social Deprivation

Certain sections of the Naga society were the priviledged ones, such as the founders of the villages. On the other hand certain professions, such as those of the 'Touchers of Luck Stones' and 'Burier' among Western Rengmas were considered to be the accursed ones.[7] The slavery prevailed among the Nagas before the formation of the Naga Hills district, especially among the Aos, Lothas, Konyaks and Phoms. The Rengmas used to buy and barter them for only two cows.[8] The slave traffic, however, was wide-spread in a large area.[9]

The prisoners of war and persons captured in raids and counter-raids,[10] fugitives,[11] bankrupts,[12] the children of the bankrupt persons sold to pay the debt,[13] and the children of the slaves used to become slaves in Naga society. The slaves did not marry in Ao area, but they were allowed free mating and their children used to became the slaves of the masters.[14] The children born of slaves were killed in the past, but the practice was abandoned later on.[15] Most of the tribals used to help their slaves by procuring mates for them for marriage. It was not uncommon to make someone slave as a punishment of theft.[16] The slaves were also procured by barter.

The slaves were given as tribute[16] or as peace-price[18] or killed to enhance the prestige of a rich man as head-hunter[19] or used as an object of sacrifice.[20] The Angamis[21] and Rengmas[22] used to procure slaves for sacrifice. The main reason of keeping slaves, however, was economic. The slaves were the prime cause of the riches of their masters.

The rich Aos invariably possessed large number of slaves. It was not unusual for a rich Ao to be surrounded by 15-20 slaves. In case of any attempt on the life of the master and the slave saving his life, the latter could hope to be emancipated from the bondage of slavery.[23] However emancipation from slavery was more or less a rare phenomenon and the bondage was invariably a permanent one. It was said that slaves became members of the master's clan, but in reality, it was not so.[24] However, the cases of slaves founding the clans were also reported.[25] Mating with slave women was prohibited among the Aos.[26]

The Nagas had many superstitions related to the slaves.[27] The dream of being sold as a slave indicated death in near future.[28] The finger of a slave was amputated to cure his Ao owner.[29] They believed that there were slaves in the next world also.[30] Aos kept little tubes of bamboo with scraps of rag stuck in the botom near the graves to represent the slaves owned by the deceased.[31]

Some Naga tribes, such as the Eastern Rengmas did not own slaves. The slaves in the Rengma area, were perhaps all from the Lotha area. As Lothas used to leave marriage prices unpaid for years, and often a youth was to find himself liable to pay the price for his mother that his father should have paid his creditors used to seize, in such case, his brothers and the sisters and sell them as slaves. The Rengmas used to barter the young man for about two cows. As the Rengmas did not purchase their own tribesmen as slaves, a good number of Lotha slaves reached them. A female slave was either re-sold or given in marriage as marriage or cohibitation with her was not allowed. A male slave, if not re-sold, was provided with a house and wife, worked for his master, protected him during war and was adopted in the clan of the master and could even inherit if there were no free born heirs.[32]

Mills has mentioned an interesting episode which shows the inner strength of the Naga tradition. A female slave and her daughter were bought by a Rengma of Tesophenyu from Lothas and kept for a long time. They, very wisely called their buyer 'father' and therefore, perforce became his adopted children and were not "sacrificed" the purpose for which they were purchased.[33]

The early British travellers observed prevailence of a large slave traffic among the Nagas.[34] Grange during his journey through Zeliang and Angami areas witnessed slave-mart. Birema was also a great mart of slaves.[35]

Structural Complexities

Exogamous clan is the unit of the tribal society of the Nagas, except for the Sema society where chieftainship exists. The clan is again very important in some Sema villages such as in Lozema where there was no chieftainship and the Angami tradition predominated.[36] The Naga villages were usually unitribal and different clans of the tribe resided in different sections (*khels*) of the same. However, there were exceptions, such as in Tobu village, where Changs and Konyaks resided in different *khels* of the village. The clan-endogamy was practised in the Wui village of the Khiamngan Nagas.[37]

The Naga social structure is not uniform. It is complex and varies from tribe to tribe. At least two reasons for the complexity are: (*i*) tribal origin from dual or multiple source, and (*ii*) fusion of races and cultures leading to formation of different tribes. Sections of some tribes use diverse languages. Some tribes have different words for mother among different sections of the tribe. The previleges of the phratries and clans differ in some cases. These indicate the diverse ethnic elements involved in the formation of the tribe concerned.

The study of the social structure and the traditions of the Nagas clearly indicate that not only the tribes but even different clans of a tribe have heterogeneous origin. Various Ao clans of Chongli and Mongsen language groups are classified under three different phratries each. The clans of the Changki group are not classified so. All the phratries and the clans do not have uniform rights in dress and social organization. Some are senior and are previleged ones, the others are not. The Chongli Ao clans are grouped under Pongen, Lungkam and Chami phratries. The Mongsen Ao clans are also grouped under three phratries which correspond to the Chongli phratries mentioned above, but they do not have specific names for them. Marriage within any clan of the phratry or the corresponding phratry is prohibited. Of the three, Pongen is regarded as the senior and Chami as the junior phratry. The former is considered to correspond to the Ang clan among the Konyaks. It has many privileges in the way of shares of meat and the right to wear certain ornaments. In the absence of the members of this phratry in a village, their rights in meat is usually held by the Lungkam phratry. The Chami phratry has the fewest privileges of all. Their inferior position, according to Mills, suggests them to be the people absorbed by the Chonglis in the course of their conquests. It needs mention that the Konyaks call the Chami Aos 'Noklang', the name given to the refugees from the Ao country who form a clan in Tamlu and Namsang.[38] Of the eight clans of the Changki group, four do not intermarry. The Lungchari clan is regarded as the senior one. One *khel* of the village, known as the 'Chongli' khel, consists of the people who fled from Changbang when that village was taken by the Lothas. The inhabitants of the *khel* have been absorbed into Changki clans, but its women, irrespective of the clan, tied their hair in Chongli style and retained Chongli pattern of tattooing.[39]

The Lothas, like Aos, have also the three-fold division of the tribe. There are three phratries divided into clans (chibo) which are in some cases split up into kindreds (mhitso, lit., tail). Although, phratry was supposed to be exogamous unit, the exogamous system started breaking down; and the marriage between different clans of the same phratry, and even between different kindred of the same clan started taking place.[40] The dual division of the Angamis into Kepezoma and Kepepfuma were supposed to be originally exogamous. Out of the two divisions (kelhu), the superiority of Kepezoma over Kepepfuma is recognized in the matter of right to start eating first during ceremonial occasions. The two Kelhus have split up into exogamous clans (thino), which in reality are the units of the Angami society. The place of 'thino' as exogamous unit was later on taken by the kindred (putsa) among the Angamis in spite of the strong disapproval of the elders of the clans. The elders profesied barren marriages or idiot and diseased children as a result of such marriages.[41] Interestingly, the same reason is given against clan (gotra) endogamy in other parts of the country.

Angamis, like most of the other Naga tribes, have eponymous clans. Their 'kelhu', 'thino' and 'putsa' are all patrilineal and patronymic. They do not show traces of Totemism.[42] But that is not true in the case of all the Naga tribes. Wotzami clan of the Semas, Kudamji of Changs, Wozukamr of the Aos and Worore clan of the Lothas point towards totemic origin.[43] The Aos have also a 'Sun clan' (anichar). The proportion of Changki clans named after plants, etc. is remarkably high. With decreasing strictness of the division into phratries the proportion of totemistic clan names increased among the Changki group. Anyway, the traces of ancient totemism are stronger among Aos than many other Naga tribes.[44]

Alapachar clan of the Pongen phratry of the Aos and Yimchenchar clan are regarded as closely connected ones. One day Yaranchang of Yimchenchar clan of Lunkam village saw an 'anget' fish spawning (muza) in a jugle spring; he brought it home, and found it turned into a boy. He named him Muzabang and kept him as a slave. In the long run, he was rewarded for some act, was freed and became founder of Alapachar clan.[45] The Rangpang clan of the Lothas, also called Mozoirangpang, is also believed to have descended from a slave or orphan.[46] Their 'Eni' clan also descended from a slave or 'jungle man'. 'Thangwe', and Sityingongnuli clans are also said to be the descendants of 'jungle men'. These 'jungle men', as usually the Lotha stories narrate, are said to be found hiding in the trees or stealing from traps. They might have been the original settlers of the land whom the migrating Nagas met.[47] As the legend says, the Chorothui clan of the Lothas originated from a stranger, claiming to descend from the sky.[48] The ancestors of Wui villagers also, similarly, descended from the sky/heaven.

Many Naga clans originated due to intra-Naga fission of ethnic elements. Sempinguli clan of the Lothas is said to be descended from Sema fugitives attaching themselves to the Nguli clan. Yanthang clan of the Lotha Nagas is descended from the Rengmas who rejoined the Lothas after the splitting up of the two tribes. The meaning of Yanthang in Lotha language is 'Rengma'. Similarly, Moyoyanthang clan descended from a band of wandering Rengmas. They are regarded as a clan of inferior status among the Lothas. They did not provide a Puthi (priest), nor did they take part in the dance at the building of a new morung. The other clans, even if of supposed extraneous origin, had equal status.[49] In this connection, it may be mentioned that Kikung clan used to claim a vague headship over the Tompyaktserre phratry, claiming that in the good old days they alone had the right to wear ivory armlets and keep mithun.[50] Among the Rengmas, the 'Azonyu' and 'Chegenyu' clans are of Sema and Angami origin.[51] New ethnic elements were introduced among the Rengmas by adoption and protection of diverse groups also.[52] Multiplication of clans in that tribe, as in other cases, was also the result of subdivision and migration.[53] The difference observed between Western and Eastern Rengmas was the result of isolation due to the separation of the latter group.

An interesting feature of the Rengmas, is the two-fold division of the tribe based on the absention from meat at harvest. Whereas a section of the tribe take meat during that occasion, the other descended from Nsenyu stock does not do so.[54]

The complex social structure of the Nagas points towards their mixed origin. This is true in the case of the individual tribes also. Their traditions do not reconcile with a homogenous origin.

REFERENCES

1. J.H. Hutton, *The Sema Nagas*, pp. 144-54.
2. J.H. Hutton, *The Angami Nagas*, p. 385 n. 2.
3. L.R.N. Srivastavas, *The Wanchos*.
4. Hutton, *The Angami Nagas*, p. 379.

5. J.P. Mills, *The Rengma Nagas*, pp. 138-40.
6. Hutton, *The Angami Nagas*, pp. 172-73.
7. Mills, *The Rengma Nagas.*
8. *Ibid.*, p. 162.
9. Elwin, Verrier, *The Nagas in the Nineteenth Century*, pp. 154, 184, 194, 200, 204, 224.
10. Mills, *op. cit.*, pp. 157, 162 n. 1.
11. *Ibid.*, p. 146.
12. Mills, *The Ao Nagas*, p. 211.
13. *Ibid.*, p. 246.
14. *Ibid.*, p. 211.
15. Rao, Professor, V. Venkata, *Slavery in North-East India, in The Thinker*, Vol. VIII, No. 1, 2; (Kohima, 1980), p. 6.
16. Hutton, *The Angami Nagas*, p. 148 n.
17. Elvin, *op. cit.* p. 207.
18. *Ibid.*, p. 326; Hutton, *The Angami Nagas*, pp. 161, 156, n. 1.
19. Mills, *The Ao Nagas*, p. 206.
20. Elvin, *op. cit.*, p. 326, Hutton, *The Angami Nagas*, p. 159; Mills, *The Rengma Nagas*, p. 161.
21. Hutton, *The Angami Nagas*, p. 159.
22. Mills, *The Rengma Nagas*, p. 161.
23. Mills, *The Ao Nagas*, p. 211.
24. *Ibid.*
25. *Ibid.*, pp. 22-23.
26. *Ibid.*, p. 211.
27. Elvin, *op. cit.*, pp. 458, 488.
28. Mills, *The Ao Nagas*, p. 292.
29. L.R.N. Srivastava, *op. cit.*, p. 98.
30. Mills, *The Ao Nagas*, pp. 200, 205, 286.
31. *Ibid.*, p. 281.
32. Mills, *The Rengma Nagas*, pp. 162-63.
33. *Ibid.*, p. 161.
34. Elvin, *op. cit.*, pp. 154, 184, 194, 200, 204, 224.
35. *Ibid.*, p. 251.
36. Hutton, *The Sema Nagas*, p. 121.
37. L.L. Yaden, *Legend of Wui, The Thinker*, Vol. 1, No. 2; Kohima, August, 1973; p. 18.
38. Mills, *The Ao Nagas*, p. 13.
39. *Ibid.*, p. 26.
40. Mills, *The Lotha Nagas*, p. 87.
41. Hutton, *The Angami Nagas*, p. 114.
42. *Ibid.*, p. 117. Hutton, *The Angami Nagas*, Appendix IV.
43. Hodson, *The Nagas of Manipur*, Hutton, *The Sema Nagas*, p. 127; Mills, *The Ao Nagas*, p. 14; *The Lotha Nagas*, p. 89; *The Rengma Nagas*, p. 11.
44. Mills, *The Ao Nagas*, pp. 24-27.

45. *Ibid.*, p. 22.
46. Mills, *The Lotha Nagas*, p. 90.
47. *Ibid.*, pp. 90-91.
48. *Ibid.*, p. 91.
49. *Ibid.*
50. *Ibid.*, p. 89.
51. Mills, *The Rengma Nagas*, p. 14.
52. *Ibid.*, p. 15.
53. *Ibid.*, p. 14.
54. *Ibid.*

10

NAGAS : THE PRE-BRITISH HISTORY

The ancient history of the Naga tribes is shrouded in obscurity. Their origin and migration is also an equally vexed question. Their legends of origin, in one hand, point towards wider linkages; on the other hand, most of the legends are shared, at best, by a few tribes only. Many of their legends point towards the common origin of the Nagas with other Indians.

Ethnic Linkages

The migration has taken place almost from every direction; from the east, south, south-east, south-west, west, north-west, north-east and the north.[1] The Naga tribes, and even their clans, are of the mixed origin.[2] Diverse connections of the Naga tribes, such as possible linguistic connections with distant Polynesians, Malays, Tahitians, Maoris and Tongans[3]; Khasis and Was[4] Kol Mon, Annam[5] Bodos,[6] Tais,[7] Igorots[8] and Indonesians[9] have been pointed out. Apart from the Indo-Mongoloid blood, they have Austric, Aryan[10] and Negrito[11] blood also. There has been massive intra-Naga diffusion of blood.[12]

Early References

The ancient Indian literature uses the term *Kirata* for the Indo-Mongoloid people which includes the Nagas also. The word finds use in the *Yajurveda, Atharvaveda, Ramayana, Mahabharata* and other literatures. Kiratas are mentioned in the Mahabharata as the best born *Kshatriyas* (warrior caste). Lord Shiva takes the garb of *Kirata*. Mother Durga is *Kirati*. '*Chirayata*' is a drug linked to the

Kiratas. The Nagas are also Kirata people. Ptolemy, the Greek traveller, geographer has used the term '*Naga Logae*'.

The Nagaland is believed to have the settlements of the tribes with Austric and Karen affinities. An Angami tradition corroborates it and says that Piphema and Kigwema were among the original Karen villages. They are said to have practised megalithic rituals and made several stone weapons, celts, basins and grinding stones. According to another tradition, the Angamis and Karens were kinsmen and they lived together. It is also reported that some other people were settled in the Sema area before their arrival. The stories of the cultivators using ornamental beads and conch-shells, and at a time the ruins of the dismantled buildings, occasionally found there, confirm the same.[13]

Hyde Clarke, on the linguistic ground (to be discussed fully elsewhere in this book), was of the opinion that the Nagas "represent sections of populations governed by a former dominant race driven up in the mountains, and there is no reason to assume that the Nagas are descendants of the dominant race, or that they have not been affected by intermarriage or immigration of the neighbouring races. They transmit in all probability the languages of the races which gave the earliest culture to India, antecedent to the Kolarians and the Dravidians."[14]

These prove the wider ethnic linkages of the Nagas. The history of the North-East is often written in isolationist frame. This does not explain the existence of long dynasties in the region.[15] The multiplicity of languages in Nagaland can also not be explained in isolationist framework.[16] Different waves of the migrations formed distinct sections even within the same tribe of Nagaland.

Relations with the Assamese

The Nagas live in the immediate neighbourhood of the Assamese people. There was huge belt of forest lying between the foot of the Naga Hills and the cultivated portion of the Brahmaputra valley when the British came. Mills is of the opinion that these forests "must have always discouraged the casual Assamese immigrant to the hills."[17] But the above-mentioned forests were of recent origin.

This happened due to the depopulation of the Brahmaputra valley during Burmese occupation. Hutton rightly observes:

> "This forest along the foot of the hills is generally regarded as of comparatively recent growth, and communication between the plains and the Naga Hills was probably much greater at an early period of history, before the Ahom invasion of Assam, than of recent years. At the same time the Aos have probably received more admixture of actual Assamese blood than most Naga tribes, and during the Burmese invasion many Assamese took refuse in the Ao country".[18] The admixture of the Shan blood among the Konyaks[19] is of comparatively later period. The same is true of the Angami-Jaintia links. Butler has mentioned "a story of the foundation of the Angami race by an exile from the court of Jaintiapur who went first to Dimapur and thence into the hills.[20] In confirmation of their links, Butler also mentions about the peculiar way the Jaintia and Angami women wear their cloths tied above the shoulders.[21]

There is not much document to detail the relationship between the Nagas and their neighbours during pre-Ahom period. Their relationship during the Ahom period is, however, well documented in the *Buranjis*. The Ahom kings enlisted the services of the Angamis and other Nagas, as well as Singphos and Kakhos in the hill regions of their armies.[22] Kacharis were the immediate neighbours of the Angamis and must obviously came in contact of each other. The legends of the Kachari Bhim Raja were equally known to the Angamis.[23]

Naga-Ahom Relations

Lt. Col. R.G. Woodthorpe had the following observations about the Nagas and their relationship with the Ahom rulers of Assam:

> "They (Nagas) have no generic term for the whole race, nor even for each of the various tribes constituting this race. A Naga when asked who he is, generally, replies that he is of such and such village, though sometimes a specific name is given to a group of villages. In the old maps of Assam, the Naga Hills immediately bordering the plains are shown as divided into

districts, the names of which as given on the maps were supposed to be the tribal names of the inhabitants of those districts. Such is, however, not the case. When the Assam Rajahs held sway over these hills, they exacted tribute from the Nagas, and for convenience in collecting this, the villages were divided into districts, or in the vernacular 'Duars', and names were arbitrarily given to these districts by the Rajahs; hence we find such names on the maps, unknown by the Nagas generally, as *'Dup-duar-ias', Pani-duar-ias, Hatigorias,* etc. Assamese names were also given to each village. The men who go down into the plains and come much into the contact with the Assamese are aware of these names, and answer to them, and even describe themselves by these Assamese names to a foreigner visiting them, but that is only because they think he will thereby understand better all about them. In the Burmese invasions of the Naga Hills many villages were looted and burned. These have been since rebuilt, and new names given to them, the old ones also being frequently restored."[24]

Similar views have been expressed by Gait about them. He wrote:

"The Nagas of the Naga Hills district have already been noticed at sufficient length, but certain tribes bearing this designation are found further east, far beyond its boundary. From the Dikhu to the Tirap, an affluent of the Burhi Dihing, the Naga tribes along the frontier are distinguished by the names of the passes through which they descend to the plains, such as Namsangia, Joboka, Tublungia, Assiringia, etc. In the time of the Ahom kings, those near the frontier used to pay annual tribute of elephants' tusks, etc., in return for which they obtained grants of land. Some of these, known as Naga *khats,* are still enjoyed. These people carry on a considerable trade in cotton and other hill produce, which they exchange for salt and rice; and they are easily kept in order by preventing them from visiting the plains, when guilty of misconduct, until reparation has been made. They quarrel amongst themselves, but it has never been our policy to meddle with their domestic feuds. Behind them are other tribes of whom we have little knowledge, except that some of them come down in the winter months to work on the tea gardens. Further east, as far as the Patkai, there are various Naga tribes who are in complete subjection to the Singphos, who seem to be quite harmless and inoffensive."[25]

In 1401, a treaty was concluded between Surumpha, the king of Mungkang and the Ahom king Sudangpha, according to which Patkai was fixed as the boundary between the two countries. The two Borgohains met on the side of the Nongnyang lake, 28 miles south-west of Margherita, and conducted the negotiations for peace. The meaning of 'Nong-nyang' is 'lake-slinking'. It is said that the statues of them have been carved in the rock there. A solemn oath of amity was also sworn, and consecrated by the cutting up of a fowl. The name 'Patkai' owes its origin to this incident. Its full name was Pat-kai-seng-kai, which means "fowl-cut-oath-sworn". The former name of the pass was 'dai-kau-rang' or 'the junction of nine peaks'.[26]

The Ao Nagas have always been friendly with the Ahom kings and they never raided the plains of Assam for head-hunting. J.P. Mills writes: "For as far back as they can remember the Aos have been friendly with the rulers of Assam, and the plains have never been used as a happy hunting-ground for head-seekers."[27] Mills further writes: "For long the Aos had maintained friendly relations with the Ahom Rajas, and several villages received grants of land in the plains in exchange for presents and promises to refrain from raiding. When, therefore, the British took over the Assam valley it was considered advisable to leave no doubt in the Nagas' minds of the reality of the change. Captain Brodie was accordingly directed to make a tour in the Ao country in 1844.[28] However, the situation changed after the collapse of the Ahom rule and the arrival of the British. The raids by the Ao Nagas on the tea gardens on the foot of the hills, in the earlier days of the tea industry, were by no means unknown. The Amguri Tea Estate, situated just below the northern end of the Chapvukong range had to maintain an armed guard, which patrolled at night, as a result of Ao raiders who used to slip into the coolie lines for heads.[29]

Other Nagas also, by and large, did not go for raiding in the plains, but when they did so, then the Ahom kings sent expeditions to force them to submission. Sudangpha subjugated Khamjang and Aiton tribes whose chiefs had again refused to pay tribute.[30] His son, Susenpha and grandson, Suhenpha had war with Tangsu Nagas and could defeat them at great loss. Akhampa Nagas came to Susenpha with a present of swords as a token of their submission.[31]

The Aitonia Nagas revolted during the reign of Suhungmung. An expedition was sent to subjugate them. They were defeated, acknowledged the supremacy of the Ahom king; sent a daughter of their chief for him and a present of four elephants as a peace offering. The Aitonia Nagas also agreed to pay a yearly tribute of axes, gongs and amber. One day, a Naga chief came to pay tribute to the Ahom king Supimpha, the father of Suhungmung. One of the king's wives praised his beauty in the hearing of the king. The king was incensed and he sent his wife to the Naga's village. She gave birth to the son there. Later on, Suhungmung discover his step-brother, created a new post of 'Barpatra Gohain' in his court and appointed him on that post. Expeditions were again sent against the Khamjang, Tablung and Namsang Nagas during 1535 and 1536 during the reign of Suhungmung. Khamjang Nagas yielded soon and paid one hundred mithuns (bisons) as fine. The other two tribes, at first inflicted a reverse on Ahom troops, and then made the submissions.[32]

The Ahoms were obstructed near Dimapur by a great body of the Naga warriors, during their march along the Doyang River to invade the Kachari king at Maibong during the 16th century. They, at first suffered defeat, ordered for more reinforcement, put into action the gallant Miri bowmen and archers to repel the Naga attack. The Nagas, at that time, were presumably assisting the Kacharis and they killed 300 coolies attached to the Ahom expedition.[33]

Gait has mentioned about an expedition against Lakma Nagas in 1650 to punish them for their raids. Another expedition was sent against them four years later. The detachment of Dafla archers also participated in the same. Ultimately, their houses and stores of grain were destroyed. Their chief came in, made his submission and agreed to pay tribute. In return, he was given a hill, the possession of which had previously been in dispute.[34] In 1665, the Banchung Nagas attacked Banpara Nagas. After being worsted, they invoked the assistance of the Ahoms. Ahoms sent expedition against the Banchung Nagas. They put up stubborn resistance but were ultimately defeated and driven off. They, however, returned again after the Ahom troops were withdrawn. A second expedition was sent. This time, it became difficult for the Ahom troops to defeat them, as they had erected a fort in the meantime. Ultimately, cannon had to be brought to defeat them. Their houses and granaries were destroyed and then they submitted.[35]

The Nagas also committed depredations in Doyang valley during the rain of King Gadadhar Singh (1681-96). An expedition, sent under Tamcheng Chinghai Phukan, searched the villages but was unable to find the culprits. He then set fire to the houses, after which the Nagas approached him and said: "We are your slaves, do not know what is right and what is wrong. We are Abors (*i.e.,* ignorant). We have given the king cause of offence. Now we shall offer two girls with two female slaves, and other articles. We hope, the Phukan will save us."[36]

The people of the Brahmaputra valley suffered immensely during the Burmese war. They were forced to seek shelter in the hills around. The Assamese, including many of the royal and noble families received shelter and material assistance in the Ao and Konyak areas during that period of crisis. Wells dug by the Ahom refugees continued to exist in the Ao area for long period. The Hill tribes also rendered assistance to the Manipuris during the Burmese invasion.[37]

REFERENCES

1. Kindly see the Chapter on the "*Origin and Migration of the Naga Tribes*."
2. Please refer: J.H. Hutton, *The Sema Nagas*, p. 125; J.P. Mills, *The Lotha Nagas*, pp. xxxv, xxxvi.
3. J.P. Mills, *The Ao Nagas,* p. 215 n. 1.
4. *Ibid.*, p. 72 n.1.
5. J.P. Mills, p. xxxvi.
6. *Ibid.*
7. *Ibid.*
8. *Ibid.*, p. xxxvii.
9. *Ibid.*, pp. xxxviii, xxxix.
10. J.H. Hutton, *op. cit.*, p. 21.
11. Bareh, H., *Nagaland District Gazetteer, Kohima district*, p. 21.
12. Kindly see the chapter on *"Making of the Naga Tribes"*.
13. Bareh, *op. cit.*, p. 15.

14. Elwin, *Nagas in the Nineteenth Century*, p. 83.
15. See *Dialogue*.
16. See the chapter on '*Naga Languages*' in this book.
17. Mills, *The Ao Nagas*, p. 4.
18. *Ibid.*, p. 4, n. 2
19. Hutton, *The Angami Nagas*, p. 384.
20. *Ibid.*, p. 20; Elwin, *The Nagas in the Nineteenth Century*, pp. 295-96.
21. Elwin, *op. cit.*
22. Hutton, *The Angami Nagas*, p. 13.
23. *Ibid.*
24. Woodthorpe, R.G., Notes on the Wild Tribes Inhabiting the So-Called Naga Hills, on our North-East Frontier of India, *Journal of the Anthropological Institute*, 1881, Vol. XI, pp. 52-53; cited by Elwin in *The Nagas in the Nineteenth Century*, p. 47.
25. Gait, Sir Edward, *The History of Assam*, p. 308.
26. *Ibid.*, p. 79.
27. J.P. Mills, *The Ao Nagas*, p. 5.
28. *Ibid.*, pp. 11-12.
29. Notes by J.H. Hutton, in J.P. Mills, *The Ao Nagas*, p. 5 n.1.
30. *Ibid.*
31. *Ibid.*, pp. 80-81.
32. *Ibid.*, pp. 81, 84, 90.
33. Bareh, *op. cit.*, p. 24.
34. Gait, *op. cit.*, pp.118-19.
35. Gait, *op. cit.*, p. 144.
36. Ahom Buranji, p. 268; cited by Lakshmi Devi in *Ahom-Tribal Relations*, Guwahati (1968), p. 68.
37. Bareh, *op. cit.*, p. 24.

11

NAGAS AND THE BRITISH

David Scot, the British representative in North-East India promised before the Anglo-Burmese war that the British would install a native prince after the war and withdraw from Assam. He thought it necessary to seek the co-operation of the people of Assam during that crucial period. However, when the time came to fulfil his declaration, after defeat of the Burmese and signing of the Yandabo Treaty on 24 February, 1826, the Governor General-in-Council did not concede to what his representative said earlier. After continuously pleading and sending memorandum, ultimately David Scot succeeded. A treaty was signed with Purandar Singh and he was allowed to rule over Upper Assam. The Ahom king was to pay Rs. fifty thousand annually which he could not pay. Ultimately, his territory was annexed in October 1938. Raja Govinda Chandra, ruler of Cachar, was murdered in 1830 and the British annexed his territory also. Thus except for the small principality of Tularam Senapati, ruling over a small portion of North Cachar and Mikir Hills, the British became the master of Assam and Cachar, Tularam's territory was also annexed in 1953.

British occupation of Assam and Cachar brought them in the neighbourhood of the Nagas and Kuki-Chin tribes. But, they did not show any desire to occupy their country due to economic reasons. The single most important reason for occupation of their country was to prevent their raids in the settled British territory and later on to prevent inter-tribal feuds. B.C. Allen, ICS, wrote:

> "It should first be premised that for the annexation of their territory the Nagas are themselves responsible. The cost of the

administration of the district is out of all proportion to the revenue that is obtained, and we only occupied the hills after a bitter experience, extending over many years, which clearly showed that annexation was the only way of preventing raids upon our villages. Had the Angami Nagas consented to respect our frontiers, they might have remained as independent as the tribes inhabiting the hills to the south of Sibsagar and Lakhimpur, but it was impossible for any civilized power to acquiesce in the perpetual harrying of its border folk."[1]

The British followed the policy of non-interference in Naga affairs for a considerably long period mainly due to two reasons:

1. The occupation and control of these areas was possible only by incurring financial loss. These areas had no prospect of gainful trade and commerce. Being traders, economic consideration was the main factor guiding the British policy in India.
2. Though the British never overlooked their ultimate interest in the overall framework of Pax Britannica, they were always cautious. The study of the trends of British annexation of North-East India clearly shows that their attitude towards the people and traditional rulers drastically changed once they gained enough strength and confidence after defeating Marathas and Sikhs, winning Sindh and consolidating their power in India.[2]

The British came in contact of the Nagas only after the collapse of the Ahom and Cachar kingdoms. It was a period of anarchy, what is called *matsya nyay* period in Indian political terminology. The over-turbulence of the Nagas, especially that of the Angamis, which the British witnessed, was due the reasons given below:

1. Collapse of the Ahom rule, resulting into state of anarchy;
2. Vacillating approach of the British towards the Naga turbulence;
3. Already existing intra-Naga ethos: the Angamis of Khonoma were already showing similar behaviour towards the Zelingroung tribes.

The British came in contact of the Angamis and Kacha Nagas during the exploration expeditions for finding out a regular communication between Assam and Manipur. The British took out several surveys in the Naga Hills starting from the year 1932. Capt. Jenkins and Pemberton set off from Manipur and traversed the Manipur and Naga Hills with a Manipuri levy of 700 soldiers and 800 coolies in January 1932. The whole party suffered much due to want of provisions. The Angami Nagas, being ignorant about the firearms, opposed their journey in most determined way. Angamis rolled stones from the summits of the hills and threw spears, did their utmost by yelling and intimidation to obstruct their advance, but all in vain. The Papoolongmaie village, consisting of 300 or 400 houses was occupied by the troops. Constant firing of musketry could only keep the Angamis at a distance. A stockade was taken at bayonet point. The village was burnt. Some Nagas were killed, many were wounded. The party could reach Mohong Dejoa in Assam with great difficulty.[3]

A second expedition, taken out by Lt. Gurdon with Manipur Raja, Gambhir Singh in 1933, encountered severe oppositions from a strong Naga confederacy. Manipuris retaliated the resistance by committing atrocities. The British had a treaty with Raja Gambhir Singh of Manipur in 1833. It provided that:

> "In the event of anything happening on the eastern frontier of the British territories, the Raja will when required, assist the British Government with a portion of his troops."

Grange undertook the journey in 1939 along Zeliangroung route from Asalu in the North Cachar Hills to Birema in the Angami area and then to Dimapur. He found the existence of slave trade in the hills. The Nagas sold the slaves at a high price to the Bengali dealers. The slave trade existed in the hills till the formation of Naga Hills district. The chiefs of Khonoma and Mezoma, two powerful Angami villages, received Grange during an eastwardly march and agreed to respect the British territory and not to commit violence anywhere outside the jurisdiction of their territory. The visit of the hills by Grange next year was not a happy one. They were subjected to stiff resistance and severe assaults; the supplies were cut off from his reach causing severe difficulties. A number of his men were lost at Punglwa. Lt. Bigge visited several Naga villages in 1941 and was received at Mezoma, Khonoma and Punglwa villages. The respective chiefs agreed to settle boundary with Manipur. There was written agreement; the Angami chiefs bordering on the British territory promised him to become tributary to the Government. They recognised Dhansiri River as the boundary. Bigge was also attacked when he approached Punglwa; but it was successfully thwarted with larger reinforcement. The agreements were violated from time-to-time. Some Nagas, of course, went upto Nowgong, the district headquarters at that time, to repair their relations with the Government. Bigge entered into treaty with the Rengmas of Borpathar in Mikir Hills. They agreed to pay the taxes to the Government. The former chiefs (called Kokotis) were restored. The Kokotis held their allegiance to the Government in the same manner as they did to the Ahoms a decade ago.[4]

The Nagas raided British territory as far as upto Cachar plains. Initially, British followed a moderate policy towards the Nagas. They were having diverse views about occupation of their country and effective control. The moderate policy followed by the British did not bring desired results. The raids continued unabated. They plundered villages, killed people, and captured and sold them as slaves. The Principal Assistant at Nowgong was of the view that a strong post should be established in the hills to control the Angamis. Accordingly Bhogchand Daroga was placed in-charge of a post. However, he was murdered soon. This followed a war with Khonoma village. The local officers wanted to take over the district administration. Supreme government did not agree to their proposals. It wanted the continuance of non-interference policy in tribal affairs. Lord Dalhosie, in his minute of 20 February 1851, recorded as follows:

> "I dissent entirely from the policy which is recommended of what is called obtaining a control, that is to say, of taking possession of these hills and of establishing our sovereignty over their savage inhabitants. Our possession could bring no profit to us, and would be as costly to us as it would be unproductive. The only advantage which is expected from our having possession of the country by those who advocate the measure is the termination of the plundering inroads which the tribes now make from the hills on our subjects at the foot of them. But this advantage may more easily, more cheaply and

> more justly be obtained by refraining from all seizure of the territory of these Nagas and by confining ourselves to the establishment of effective means of defence on the line of our frontier..."
>
> "Hereafter, we should confine ourselves to our own ground; protect it as it can and must be protected; not meddle in the feuds or fights of these savages; encourage trade with them as long as they are peaceful towards us and rigidly exclude them from all communications either to sell what they have got or to buy what they want if they should become turbulent or troublesome."[5]

Initially, it was the practice for some years to look to Tularam and the Raja of Manipur to exact reparation for the raids committed by the turbulent Angami Nagas, and the tendency was to encourage the Raja of Manipur to extend his dominion over the whole area between the Doyang and Dhansiri. The British Government relied too much on its treaty with Manipur mentioned earlier. The policy was a failure. The British Government sent ten military expeditions in the hills between 1835 and 1851. After the inauguration of the policy of non-interference, in the very first year, there were twenty-two raids in which 178 persons were killed, wounded or carried off.[6]

This step proved to be counter-productive. Raids continued. There were 19 raids by the Angamis between 1852 and 1865 in which 232 British subjects lost their lives. Jenkins, the Commissioner of Assam asked for the abandonment of non-interference policy in 1862. The situation indeed became awkward for the local officers, and the Commissioner of Assam reported as follows to the Lt. Governor in 1862:

> "It is not creditable to our Government that such atrocities should recur annually with unvarying certainty, and that we should be powerless alike to protect our subjects or to punish the aggressors. It is quite certain that our relations with the Nagas could not possibly be on a worse footing than they are now. The non-interference policy is excellent in theory; but the Government will probably be inclined to think that it must be abandoned."[7]

Sir Cecil Beadon, Lt. Governor of Bengal concurred with the views of the Chief Commissioner and urged the Government of India to re-orient its policy towards the Nagas. He was of the opinion that no line of posts, however strong, could guard the plains from the incursions of the Hill tribes. He said that the only alternative was "to re-assert our authority over them, and bring them under a system of administration suited to their circumstances, and gradually to reclaim them from habits of lawlessness to those of order and civilization." Their pressure worked and the Government approved the establishment of a strong central station. The officer-in-charge of the station was to maintain friendly relation with the Nagas. Lt. Gregory established, in pursuance of the above decision, headquarters at Samaguting (Chumukedima) in 1866. The district included a small part of Naga inhabited area and parts of Rengma and Mikir Hills transferred from Nowgong district. Earlier, fringe of Naga Hills formed part of Asalu sub-division, which was abandoned after establishment of the district. The district headquarters was transferred from Samagooting to Kohima in 1878. Plains portion of the district was transferred back to Nowgong and Sibsagar in 1898. Dimapur was re-transferred to Naga Hills district by a notification dated 19-11-1930. In 1923, Digar Mouza was transferred to North Cachar Hills subdivision.

Angamis were the most turbulent tribe among the Nagas. The last Angami rebellion lasted for 6 months during 1879. This uprising culminated into murder of Deputy Commissioner, Damant at Khonoma followed by seize of Kohima. The rebellion was crushed; but the raids in other parts of the districts did not stop. The history of Naga Hills district is full of incidents of raids and counter-raids by the villages and punitive actions of the government till the tribes learnt pacific ways of life.

Mokochung sub-division was added in 1879. Earlier, the sub-divisional headquarters was located at Wokha, which was established in 1875. The country was incorporated within the British jurisdiction in 1889 with full concurrence of the people, who had claimed protection against the onslaughts of the more war-like tribes from across the Dikhu. The observation of Government of India is worth quoting here:

> "It is not intended that the system of political control should be generally and definitely abandoned but in this particular part of

the country, where the people are themselves willing to pay revenue in return for protection, there is no sufficient reason why their wishes should not be acceded to."

In general, government did not like to extend the area of political control, but wherever it was done, house-tax was imposed on the incorporated tract which should "pay its own expenses". In spite of government's unwillingness, more areas were incorporated upto first two decades of the current century. The group of Sema villages was incorporated soon after establishment of Mokochung subdivision. More and more villages in present day Phek, Zunheboto and Mokochung district were gradually brought under political control. Siromi, a large Sema village was added to the district during 1900.

In spite of local officers urging to do so, the Supreme government did not like to bring Tuensang district under settled administration on the plea that men and funds were not available.

From 1902 under the provisions of special Order-in-Council, the Tuensang villages were administered by the Governor General of India to apply any British law to them. The Government of India Act of 1935, continued this arrangement and Tuensang was defined as a Tribal area.

There was gradual extension of Government control in Tuensang area in the next decades through punitive expeditions and goodwill tours of the Deputy Commissioner of the Naga Hills district in non-administered tract. A post was established in Wakching village after 1913. Punitive expedition was sent to Chinglong due to their participation in a raid, in which 120 Nagas were killed by Chinglong raiders.

In 1906, Sema villages east of Tizu were incorporated in Mokokchung subdivion. In 1908, a large number of Konyak villages and in 1927 a Phom village and some other villages were added to Mokokchung subdivision. All these additions were done most reluctantly during these decades and pace of incorporation of new areas under active administrative was very slow.

The Naga Hills district, which became part of Nagaland, first as a centrally administered territory and then as the 16th state of Indian Union was fully annexed upto nineteen twenties by the British and Tuensang apart from friendly tours and punitive expeditions remained unadministered. The annexation was done slowly, haltingly and hesitatingly. At one point, British even wanted to offer as much part of Naga Hills to Manipur kings as possible. Sir Robert Reid, the Governor of Assam (1937-48) succinctly summed up the process in the following words:

> "...the process of penetration went on, inexorably if irregularly. It was impossible to draw a line as the boundary of our area of control and to say that we should be blind and deaf to all that went on across that line. Trans-frontier Nagas raid our administered villages, the latter are involved in dispute with the former, head hunting and massacres go on just across the border and under the very noses of our officers. In such conditions local officers inevitably, and with reason, clamour for forward policy. The Chief Commissioner sometimes supports them, sometimes he does not. The Government of India is nearly always reluctant. But the frontier moves forward."[8]

The British frontier gradually moved eastward on one excuse or another. As the Chief Commissioner wrote in his letter of 8 August 1901:

> "Where there is an ethnological boundary it will be said that a further extension is necessary in order to secure a good natural and geographical boundary. When the boundary is a natural one an ethnological frontier is declared to be the best. When the boundary is a stream it is proposed to push it on to the top of the mountain ridge beyond. When the watershed has been reached it will be found that political considerations require an extension to the bed of the next river below and so on *ad infinitum.*"[9]

The British attitude towards the further annexation of the hills is reflected in the following observation of A.W. Davis, Deputy Commissioner of the Naga Hills district, made in 1907. He said "We shall have no real peace until we have absorbed the whole Hill area between this and the Chindwin. This can be done gradually and economically. Hill country between Assam and Burma is an anomaly."[10] The Government of Assam also saw the benefit of annexation. It was of the opinion that punitive expeditions launched in the past had not produced the desired results "whereas in areas of political control the protection of the British Government has converted scenes of chronic murder and intensive feud to peace and agriculture." Sir Archdale Earle, the Chief Commissioner of Assam, said in 1914 that the process of expansion would have to be continued, "until the whole of the country between Assam and Burma has been taken over". The discovery of coal to the east of Dikhu aroused commercial interest and the support of the British Government in London.[11]

Naga Attitude Towards the British

The attitude of the Nagas towards the British drastically changed after some time. They enormously helped the allied and British forces during the Second World War, which was also fought at Kohima. The following excerpt would illustrate the kind of help extended to the British:

> "A Naga Government interpreter located a Japanese ammunition party of nine men and organised a band of villagers who surrounded and captured them. This is typical of the sort of assistance given. Another interpreter, hearing of an advanced Japanese patrol of 15 men, guided a British patrol to ambush and capture or destroy the party, which he assisted in doing himself. One Naga undertook a night trip behind the Japanese lines in Kohima village and its outskirts and came back with detailed information, which enabled troops to push into Kohima village and turn the whole Japanese position. Another brought back information so accurate that targets on the Japanese supply line could be pin-pointed and destroyed from the air with the greatest precision."[12]

William Slim acknowledged their contribution thus: "The gallant Nagas whose loyalty, even in the depressing times of the invasion, never faltered, despite floggings, torture, execution and the burning of the villages, they refused to aid the Japanese in anyway or to betray our troops. Their active help to us was beyond virtue or praise. They guided our column, collected informations, ambushed every petrol, carried over supplies and brought in our wounded under the heaviest fire, and they being the gentlemen refused all payments."[13]

Haimendorf has also described their contribution eloquently.[14] Hundreds of people died in Southern Nagaland and Naga villages of Manipur due to spread of epidemics after the war. There was starvation in interior villages due to shortage of foodstuff. But the war had tremendous impact on them as it exposed them to most modern technology. It needs mention that a labour force, consisting of 1000 Semas, 400 Lothas, 200 Rengmas, 200 Aos and 200 Changs and others, went to France during First World War. They came back to Naga Hills with exposure and new ideas. The importance of this factor in the modernization of Naga Society can not be under-estimated.

British Plan to Separate the Hills

Some British officers were secretly trying to separate the hills of India and Burma and form a separate political unit. Robert Neil Reid, the then Governor of Assam, J.H. Hutton, the Deputy Commissioner of Naga Hills district and J.P. Mills, the Adviser to the Governor subscribed to the idea of separation, and strongly favoured creation of North-East Frontier Province under British protection, Andrew Clow, the Governor of Assam and Sir Reginald Coupland, a British constitutional expert, favoured the formation of Crown Colony, comprising hills of North-East India and Burma. According to Coupland, "the inhabitants of both areas are alike in race and culture, and in no sense belonged to the Indian or Burman nation". There were certainly some takers of such ideas among the tribals of North-East India. The freedom came too early for the British officers and so they could not get their plan of separation materialized.[15]

The impression about the formation of 'Crown Colony' was getting currency and becoming strong. The Government of India found it necessary to clarify the matter and therefore issued a Press Note, which said:

> "The attention of the Government of India have been drawn to allegation that schemes are under consideration for the separation of the Assam hill areas from India and their constitution into a separate Colony or State. There is no truth in these allegations and no such scheme is being considered. Nor is there any intention, at present, to create a new Hill Province.

> The creation of a new province would require Parliamentary legislation and no such proposal would be considered prior to the convening of the Constituent Assembly.[16]

The attitude of the British officers changed. They reconciled to the idea of the hills remaining in Assam and India. Sir Andrew Clow, Governor of Assam, visited Mokokchung in January 1947 and met the leaders of all the northern Naga tribes and explained to them the coming constitutional changes. He advised them "to seek to form part of the province, but to retain matters of local concern in their own hand." He said:

> "The British Raj is being withdrawn shortly, and the future Government of India, including Assam and its hills, will be a matter for the peoples of the land to decide. The Constituent Assembly, which is charged with working out the plans for the future, has already started its work in Delhi, and it will have to consider, in due course, the position of the hill peoples. They should, therefore, themselves be thinking over the question and form their own conclusions regarding what they want. It is not practicable for the Naga tribes or even the Nagas as a whole to set themselves in a separate State or States (as some of them want) or even as a (separate) province of India. If they did they would always remain poor and backward and could not supply even the inadequate services they already enjoy. They would, therefore, be well advised to seek to from part of the province, but to retain matters of local concern in their own hand. Even in the plains, many matters of local concern are run by the people of the district concerned, and here, where their custom and culture differ so much from those of the plains, they could reasonably claim a larger sphere for local authority, including control of their own land and conservation of such authority as is traditionally theirs."[17]

Freedom Movement and the Nagas

The British did every thing to isolate the Nagas. Fortunately, the Naga inhabited areas did not go unrepresented in the Freedom Movement. Jadunang, a Zeliangroung Naga, and his niece Gadiliu, popularly known as Rani Gadiliu (She was called Rani by Pt. Nehru), started Khampai Movement and fought against the British. Jadonang was hanged. Rani Gadiliu was sentenced to life imprisonment in 1933, and was released only in 1946. Rani went underground in 1960 and re-activated the Khampai Movement as counterweight to underground movement led by Phizo. The latter movement could grow root in Zeliangroung area only after her coming over-ground in January 1966.

The British did, practically, nothing for the development of the Nagas. The only two High Schools in the Naga Hills district were started during early 1940s; Naga Hospital at Kohima was started after Second World War. A few schools, including the Middle Schools were run by the Baptist Missionaries. Massive development started in the Naga inhabited areas only after the independence, and more so after the Statehood.

REFERENCES

1. B.C. Allen, *Assam District Gazetteer* (1906); quoted by Hokishe Sema in *Emergence of Nagaland,* p.15.
2. B.B. Kumar, *Trends of British Annexation in North-East India,* New Delhi (1994), pp. 6, 29, 33.
3. Moffat Mills, A.J., *Report on the Province of Assam,* 1854, p. cxl; reproduced by Elwin in *Nagas in the Nineteenth Century,* p. 114.
4. Bareh, Dr. H., *The Nagaland District Gazetteer, Kohima district,* pp. 26-27.
5. Mackenzie, A., *History of the Relations of the Government with the Hill Tribes of the North-East Frontier of Bengal,* Calcutta (1884), p. 114.
6. Gait, Sir Edward, *A History of Assam,* Guwahati, 6th edition, 1994; pp. 298-99.
7. Mackenzie, *op. cit.,* p. 116.
8. Reid, Sir Robert; *History of the Frontier Areas Bordering on Assam from 1883-1941;* Shillong (1942), pp. 100-101.
9. *Ibid.,* p. 131.
10. Quoted by Prakash Singh, *op. cit.,* pp. 22-23.
11. *Ibid.,* p. 23.
12. J.H. Hutton, *Problems of Reconstruction in the Assam Hills,* Man in India, Vol. XXVI, No. 2, June 1946, p. 100.
13. Quoted in *Nagaland,* p. 26.
14. *The Naked Nagas,* p. 26.
15. B.B. Kumar, *Re-Organization of North-East India,* p. 25.
16. Hokishe Sema, *op. cit.,* cited on p. 82.
17. *Ibid.,* p. 83.

12

CHRISTIANITY AMONG THE NAGAS

It was the decision of the Christian Missionaries of India that they should avoid mutual conflict and overlap in their activities in this country. Accordingly, Assam was assigned to the Protestant Churches and the Naga Hills district of Assam fell to the American Baptist Church.[1] Rev. M. Bronson, the first missionary among the Nagas, went and worked among Hindu Vaishnavite Nocte Nagas of Namsang in Tirap district of the present Arunachal Pradesh during 1835-40. He, however, could not succeed in his effort and had to leave the place very soon.[2] It goes to the credit of Sibsagar Baptist Mission to get the first Naga Christian convert—an Ao Naga—for the new religion in 1851. Nine more Nagas were converted in 1872 due to the pioneering work of Mr. Subongmeren, an Ao Naga convert and Mr. Godhula, an Assamese evangelist.[3] This encouraged Dr. E.W. Clark, the missionary at Sibsagar, to visit Molungyimchen village on 18 December, 1872. 15 persons were baptised by him on December 23, 1872, leading to the first foundation of a Church on the soil of Naga Hills. A year later, the Christian population was separated and settled in a new village, Molungyimsen, three miles to the north of the old one, Molungyimchen (Deka Haimong).[4] The first Baptist Mission Centre was established there in 1876. It was shifted to Impur in October 1894.

Impur Mission Centre continued to work in trans-Dikhu region among the Changs, Phoms, Konyaks, Sangtams Yimchungrus and Khiamngans even after the Independence and no American Baptist Centre was established in their area till 1955 when the foreign missioneries had to leave India.[5] Apart from the Impur Centre started by Rev. Clark, Kohima Mission Centre was started by

Rev. C.D. King in 1880. The first Angami was Baptised in 1885. The work at Wokha was started in 1885 by W.E. Witter. Kohima Centre looked after the work in Angami, Sema, Rengma and Chakhesang areas, and Wokha Centre in Lotha area. In 1913, Rev. Tanquist visited the Sema area and the Sema Association was formed in 1922.

Progress of evengelization remained very slow, except in few areas, even upto Independence in 1947. The membership of the church among the Aos rose to seventy-nine by 1885-86.[6] There were 22 Chang, Kalyo-Kenyu (Khiamngan), 18 Phom and three Yimchungru communities in Tuensang district in 1950 with only 1800 Church members and only 252 Changs were converted to Christianity in that particular year.[7] Rapid conversion started only after Independence. The Christian population increased by 99.44 per cent during 1951-61. It further increased by 76.29 per cent during 1961-71. Percentage of Christian population to total population during 1971, 1981 and 1991 was reported to be 66.76 per cent, 80 per cent and 90 per cent respectively.[8]

The Ao Naga missionaries took lead in evangelical work among trans-Dikhu tribes. In 1933, Tamlu Baptist Church was formed in Konyak area by Rev. Longri Ao and Rev. Subongwati. This was a year after a Konyak was converted in the Ao area. Around 1936, the Baptist Mission work started in the Sangtam area and the Sangtam Association was formed in 1946. The first persons to be baptised among Changs and the Phoms were in 1941 and 1943 respectvely.[9]

The Baptist Churches and the Associations of Nagaland work under Nagaland Baptist Church Council (NBCC). The latter is affiliated through the Council of Baptist Churches of North-East India (CBCNEI) and the Baptist Union of India to the Baptist World Alliance, headquartered at Washington. Nagaland Baptist Women's Union is the women's wing. 'Home Mission Board' works for the intensified proselytization campaign among the backward tribes, and 'Nagaland Foreign Baptist Mission' for evangelization abroad.

Baptist Mission started some schools, prominent among which were the schools at Impur and Kohima. Today, they have a Baptist College at Kohima. The missionaries initiated the use of Roman script for the Naga langauges. Rev. E.W. Clark authored Ao Naga Dictionary (Calcutta, 1991). He taught in a primary school for two hours each week-day in the morning without affecting his preaching work. He also engaged himself in the production of Christian literature, hymns in Ao language, and preliminary text-books. Mrs. Clark prepared Ao language Grammar (Shillong, 1893), assisted her husband in preaching and teaching and started a school for Naga girls. Rev. W.E. Witter produced frist grammar and vocabulary of the Lotha language. Mrs. Witter, apart from helping her husband in his missionary work, took Sunday School classes in Assamese. Rev. W. Pettigrew prepared Grammar and the Dictionary of the Tangkhul Naga language of Manipur (Shillong, 1918). The Bible was translated and published in most of the Naga languages.

The first qualified medical missionary among the Nagas was Dr. S.W. Rivenburg, who joined Molung Yimsen Mission in 1885 and left soon after for Kohima. Dr. Bailey came after him. The missionary Doctors of Jorhat supervised the work of Impur dispensary after his departure. The dispensary remained in the charge of a trained Ao compounder after Dr. Bailey's departure. Another missionary hospital was running at Aizuto in the Sema area.

The attitude of the Nagas towards conversion varied from tribe to tribe. Some readily accepted the new faith, whereas some others, such as the Angami Nagas continued to resist and did not show disposition towards conversion from the very beginning.[10] In the beginning, warriors and priests among the Changs opposed it and Bumbu section (commoners and adopted sections) accepted it readily.[11]

The attitudes of the British officers towards Christianity differed from person to person. While some of them were critical of the *modus operandi* of the missionaries, most of them favoured it. Some favoured it keeping the interest of the British empire in mind. J. Johnstone writes:

> "Late General Dalton, C.S.I., when Commissioner of Chota Nagpur did his utmost to aid Christian Mission among the wild Kols; his argument being like mine, that they wanted a religion and that were they Christians, they would be a valuable counterpoise in time of trouble to the vast non-Christian population of Bihar. In the same way it cannot be doubted, that a large population of Christian hillmen between Assam and Burmah would be a valuable prop to the state."[12]

David Scot, the first Commissioner of Assam was of the opinion that, "rude tribes were more likely to profit by the teachings of the gospels".[13] The next Commissioner of Assam, Major Jenkins held similar view that, "the tribes on the Assam frontier should be brought within the scope of missionary activities as early as possible as the influence of persons skilled in the languages of these tribes, and devoting all their time and attention to humanize these rude races could not fail of being useful to us and to them." It was through latter's attempt that Rev. Nathan Brown of the American Baptist Mission arrived in Sadiya in 1836 to take up missionary work in Assam.[14]

William Robinson, in 1841, wrote: "hoped, that by the blessing of Divine Providence through the efforts of these excellent men, the Nagas, who from time immemorial have been the scorn and prey of their more civilized neighbours, may shortly begin to emerge from the dark barbarism which now renders the tribe of each hill an enemy to that of the next, and has hitherto prevented an Alpine tract of great natural resources and high fertility, from supporting more than a very scanty population of savages in a state of discomfort and privation".[15]

The British administrators were averse to continuance of Naga religion and culture. A person like E.A. Gait perceived tribal religion as simply the "superstitions of their forefathers" and "demon worship"[16]. For John Butler, the Nagas were "so thoroughly primitive, and so independent of religious prepossessions".[17] J. Johnstone was of the opinion that Nagas had no religion and "we might give them our own". He feared, otherwise, that "they would sooner or later become debased Hindoos or Mussulmans".[18]

Hutton feared "early denationalization" of the Lothas "between the upper and the nether mill-stones of Christianity, as taught by the American Baptist Mission, and Hinduism, as practised by the Nepali settler or by the Assamese who are the neighbours of the Lotha on the plains side". It was, as he observed, "unpleasantly common thing to have Lotha ceremonies and the officials of the Lotha hierarchy spoken of in spurious terms of Hindiusm." Hutton found the Hindu tendency most noticeable in the south. One of the interpreters of his office, supposed to be the natural guardian and exponent of tribal customs, came to him and asked for leave for the

"Lakshmi Puja", by which he meant "Rangsikam" festival.[19] Needless to say, it was possible to put full stop to such tendencies very soon. The elements of Naga culture were also tabooed in due course by the Baptist Christianity.

The ways and means followed by the missionaries for preaching Christianity are given below:

(*i*) The study and use of the local languages,
(*ii*) Simple preaching,
(*iii*) Use of student groups and gospel teams,
(*iv*) Scripture translation and other literary works,
(*v*) Village schools and boarding houses,
(*vi*) The role of native evangelists,
(*vii*) Medical work,
(*viii*) The witness of the life of the missionaries, and
(*ix*) The Naga love for music and songs.[20]

The other factors, which reportedly influenced the Baptist Missionary work in the area were the extension of the British rule in the neighbouring areas, the nature of the tribals and their readier response to the Christian message, Dr. Clark's role as the mission strategist and the moments of revival.[21] Christianity was the religion of the colonial masters; it gave it a status and the psychological benefit. Christian converts with education in missionary schools were financially well-placed as they got jobs and status. In spite of the same, the conversion was not a smooth affair and the missionaries resorted to other means also for conversion discussed below.

The reasons of rapid conversion of the Aos into Christianity, given by Mills, were (*i*) the expectation of miraculous results due to a lamentably common frame of mind, where they regarded Christianity as a sort of patent medicine, a dose of which without much after treatment will cure him of and protect him from all ills bodily and spiritually in this world and the next",[22] and (*ii*) the fear of hell-fire.[23] Mills has noted the following interesting conversation:

> "A significant remark was made to me one day by an elderly man. He had for long a sore on his foot and I asked him how he

was? He replied: "I have become a Christian, but my foot is no better." On another occasion I expressed surprise at a man who almost alone in his village was not a Christian. He said: "I used to be rich and I was told I should become richer still if I become a Christian. I became one. But instead of growing richer I grew poorer. So I have given it up and I am getting on quite nicely again now." Yet another man who longed for children was assured by an Ao pastor that he would become a father if he would only be baptized. These are examples and not isolated instances".[24]

The fear of hell-fire continued to trouble most of the non-Christian Nagas as the missionaries constantly taught them that the heathens shall be doomed to the terrible fate and shall continuously burn in the great fire of hell. Many Nagas continued to follow traditional faith throughout their life and convert to Christianity in old age to avoid burning in the hell-fire. However, all were not afraid of that terrible fate. Mills mentions about one such case:

> "By no means all trouble at the thought of Hell. A Chang, when talking to me recently of the visit to him of some Ao pastors, said 'who knows whether what they say is really true? No one has come back from the dead to tell them what the next world is like. Even if their words are true am I a coward that I should fear to join my father and my mother and suffer whatever torments they may be suffering? If they can bear, cannot I?"[25]

An important factor, which helped in easy acceptance of Christianity was the relative ease of the entry and re-entry in its fold. Mills observation about the same is worth-quoting:

> "A religion so easily assumed can be as easily discarded, and one finds many men who have changed their faith as often as seven or eight times, or even more. A man will become a (nominal) Christian and be baptised. Then his soul yearns for madhu and since anyone who touches alcohol is expelled from the Baptist Community, he often goes a whole hog and joins the non-Christians again. Later, he may change his mind, give up his madhu and heathen practices and be re-admitted into the Baptist Church. The idea that a man can change his religion is

a novel one, to an Ao and entirely foreign to his old way of thinking. Whatever may be the fault of the Ao religion, everyone till the missionaries came believed in it, and it permeated every part of life. Now side by side with sincere Christianity and sincere Animism there has arisen Agnosticism and total lack of any religion. How serious the evil is may be judged from the fact that in the census of 1921, 1180 persons returned themselves as "sitters in the middle", people with no religion at all. They consisted of people, who had left or been turned out of the Baptist community, and who had as yet neither gravitated back to animism, nor been received again into the Church. These alone are equal to more than one-eighth of the total number of Christians. But they are only the people whom the census caught on the way, as it were between the two religions. Add to them the far greater number who have definitely returned to their old religion, or who have re-embraced Christianity after one or more lapses, and one can realise the commonness of an unstable; or indeed, at times flippant attitude of mind."[26]

Conversion created acute "two world" situation in Naga society. The situation, however, drastically changed after dwindling of the number of the followers of the traditional religion. A large number of Baptist Christians openly declare that they drink. The educated ones show greater awareness and sympathetic attitude towards their culture and cultural institutions. They have started observing old festivals, though in modified forms.

The missionaries had scant understanding of the Naga Culture and traditions. They thought them to be totally heathenistic and undesirable and acted against them. They caused immense damage to the tribal culture; many institutions received death blows at their hands. "The disappearance of the young men's house or Morung is due to the fact that from the very onset the missionaries frowned on these as being in their opinion dens of vice where singing, dancing, drinking and sex were the only pre-occupations."[27] Due to its disappearance, the Nagas suffered immense social, cultural and architectural loss. Naga folk-music, folk-lore, folk-dance festivals and many other social activities were considered to be part of the animistic society and purposely undermined. The missionaries lacked the capacity to differentiate between Animism and culture; they lumped together animistic beliefs and aspects of culture, resulting almost in the extinction of some unique aspects of Naga Culture.[28] The Baptist Missionaries, like missionaries throughout the world are in the habit of translating the Animist gods into English as "satan". This has been done in the case of the Nagas also.[29] It, however, needs mention that many Animist gods are far from having the qualities of Satan, and rather than being malicious, are definitely benevolent.

Two factors influenced the *modus operandi* of the early missionaries, which were: (*a*) distorted impression about the indigenous culture due to their colonial mind set, and (*b*) their pre-occupation with the increasing number of the converts. Due to the first factor, everything related to the Naga culture and society was savage and barbaric. For Dr. Clark, the new surrounding appeared no better than "a leap out of the world and a plunge into barbarism".[30] The first impression of Mrs. Clark was not different. She wrote: "When we entered 'A Corner of India' (the Naga Hills) the darkness seemed impenetrable".[31] S.A. Perrin, another missionary, wrote in 1899: "Here (at Impur), we are on the edge of world, surrounded as we are by such dark and dense heathenism."[32] With such frame of mind, naturally, they thought it to be their Christian duty to put stop to all these "heathen practices".[33]

The missionaries were to report to the Board about the success of their labour in terms of the number of adherents.[34] Naturally, their pre-occupation with the task of increasing the number of adherents made them unimaginative regarding questions concerning how the story of Jesus could be given new expression"[35] in the context of the local culture. For many pastors, the number of converts was important irrespective of the bait used.[36] There are examples when the pastor resigned his post because he had baptized the entire village and regarded his task to be over. All the persuasion for withdrawal of his resignation as his work had just started were unsuccessful. This illustrates the attitude and outlook of the persons who very earnestly and enthusiastically worked for winning over the converts and considered it to be their ultimate achievement.

The missionaries banned local beer, dress, folk-songs, folk-tales, local festivals, gennas, Morungs and most of the items of the local culture considering them to be part of the heathen religion and practices. "More Clothes" were advocated at the very first rally of the Christians. The Naga converts used Assamese costumes of jacket and body-cloth.[37] According to Mrs. Clark, the Naga dress was "the exhibition of taste so degrading and repulsive."[38] Perrin refused to baptise a certain Kilep Ao for not obeying the dress prescription. The latter, however, became enthusiastic on his own and started a "Christian Reform Movement" with the help of the villagers and was baptized later on."[39]

As a step to reform the Church, the American missionaries, Perrine and Haggard brought total prohibition of liquor in 1894. But it was difficult for a Naga to go without the same. The question of drinking occupied a central place in the Baptist communities. Clark observed:

> "We missionaries are accused of meddling with their (the people's) food. Of our converts the great question of 99 of a hundred is that of giving up rice-beer not a question of choice between the old faith and the new."[40]

The Baptist Missionaries banned many things, but nothing loomed so large in Naga mind as that of *madhu* (local liquor, rice-bear, job's tear beer). The Christian community voted in favour of drinking and was officially disbanded on 19 August, 1894. Haggard described the disbandment thus:

> "They (the people), in full light, voted not to give it up. I put it to my (this was a pundit I had a shortwhile at Molung) Christian pundit, "Will you choose Christ or the 'Yi' (the tribal word for rice-beer in Chongli dialect of Ao Naga)? He said, "I must have my 'Yi'. "I do not believe you ask me to baptize a man who would make such a stand and choice as that. Certainly, if you did, I would cut off my hand before I would comply. I believe it is absolutely necessary for this people to totally abstain, if it never had been for any other."[41]

Clark's attitude on this dramatic turn of events was one of caution and suppressed approval. He stated:

> "Perhaps I should say that I never approved of or had any hand in the disbandment of Molung Church. But for certain reasons I did withdraw all opposition."[42]

Even some missionaries also did not like this wholesale rejection of Naga culture. Supplee, himself a missionary, wrote:

> "When we speak of an encounter between the Gospel and a given culture (say, the Naga Culture), it should be borne in mind, that the encounter is between persons, and not between the Good News and a culture in the abstract. Therefore, it was not so much the Gospel message that met the Naga way of life, but the American Baptist (Christian) missionaries."[43]

Taboos and gennas were the common features of all the traditional religions, including that of the Nagas. For many casual converts, therefore, the bans "meant nothing more than the exchange of one set of taboos for another." Earlier they observed gennas which was replaced by Sabbath. The old food taboos, similarly, were substituted by prohibition. However, the issue involved in this case was of wholesale rejection of a culture and therefore, a different one. Professor William C. Smith (Assistant Professor of Sociology in University of Southern California, and a former member of the American Baptist Mission in Ao area) had personal experience of the local situation. He wrote:

> "Familiarity with missionary attitude and practices, which are all too characteristic makes inevitable the conclusion that there is entirely too much negation, too much taboo and too little positive."[45]

According to professor Haimendorf, the Christian Missionaries were responsible for the adulteration of Naga culture. The discontinuance of the feasts of merit, the loss of the knowledge of wood-carving as an art and means of subsistence, replacement of the rice-beer for tea were the negative developments.[46] The old clan solidarity has weakened. The clan and not the family was the real binding factor in the Naga villages. It was compulsory for the individuals to obey the clan elders. The individuals had no other way than to put up with all the curbs imposed on them by the clan elders. This accounted for the stern discipline and unity within the clan. With the growing individualism, placing personal interests over those of the clan has resulted into disintegration and indiscipline. The spirit of sacrifice and unity at all costs have disappeared and with these are vanishing some of the most noble traits of Naga character.[47] The westernization also owes its origin to the same source.

Frequent cases of internal division and tension were reported soon after the inception of Christianity among the Nagas. Dr. Clark himself founded new Christian village to settle converts from Molungyimchen and Merangkong villages.[48] Rengma Christians founded 'New Tsemenyu' village.[49] Milada Ganguli has described the situation in the Chang village of Chingmei thus:

> "The little church below the pastor's hut is no longer big enough to accommodate them. If they do not arrive an hour before the service is due to begin, they find the few square metres inside packed with worshippers, and have to join the growing throng outside under the trees to listen to the preaching and sing hymns. Therefore, they now hope that the old Morung occupying the most beautiful spot in the whole village will be demolished and in its place a big church built. They argue that the Morung no longer serves any purpose since making wars has been forbidden and a church is best built on a hill top, as only there can it be seen even from distant surroundings."
>
> "Thus there developed in Chingmei two camps—one made up of obstinate clansmen, who stubbornly adhere to the customs of their ancestors fearing that if they give them up they will lose favour with their tribal gods; and the other camp made up of believers of the new faith. These enthusiasts along with their pastor are doing their best to increase the number of Christians, gain majority in the village and thus force their heathen relatives to allow them to demolish the Morung and replace it with a Church."[50]

Mills has compared the behaviour of the Christians and the non-Christians among the Aos. According to him, "Certainly on the whole Christian Aos are more truthful and honest than the non-Christians and they are less vindictive and quarrelsome, save in matters of religion, and less keen on getting the offender punished as heavily as possible when sinned against."[51] He also observed that there were more pre-marital liaisons and strict incestuous taboo observation among Animists,[52] stricter post-marital relations and loss of sense of humour among the Christians,[53] and frequent divorces on trivial reasons among both.[54]

All sections of the Naga tribals were not equally receptive to the Christianity and modern education. There is a saying among the Changs that "only the lazy go to the schools." In many cases a person from the lower social status got converted, received English education and job, and thus became a member of the neo-previledged section of the society. Thus these factors not only worked as 'status equilizers' but also catalysed the status re-mix.[55] It caused social tension and conflict in the beginning. Gradually, however, the control and dominance of the Christians in politics and administration was total. It helped rapid conversion. Due to obvious reason, the conversion was more rapid in post-Independence period and majority of the Nagas became Christians only then.

Christianity always remained a favoured religion of the underground Nagas. Rather, they went a step ahead, and when the entry of the Roman Catholic Church in Nagaland was vehemently opposed by the Baptists, the Underground Naga Army abducted five Catholics from Zhamai in the Chakhesan area on 16 August, 1967, and another seven from the same village on 29 November, 1967. The Yehzabo (Constitution) of the 'Naga Federal Government' speaks of 'Nagaland for Christ'. It states that Baptist Christianity and Naga religion 'alone' be recognized.[56] It needs mention that majority of the underground Nagas are themselves Baptists.

One can never forget the commendable role played by the Baptist Church of Nagaland and the Churches of Mizoram in bringing peace to the strife-torn states. At the same time, we cannot ignore the use of terror in Tripura and Arunachal Pradesh for forcible conversion into Christianity. The NSCN(IM), which has virtually taken over the two districts—Tirap and Changlang of Arunachal Pradesh, is forcing several thousand Buddhists (and Hindu Vaishnavite Nocte Nagas) to become Christians. "The NSCN militants have issued a decree to villagers in Tirap and Changlang districts to convert to Christianity or face capital punishment". Many have fled to avoid conversion; thousand have become Christians.[57] In Tripura, the story is not different. Tribal Hindus were forced to abandoned Saraswati Puja, to say the least.

When a large number of people were killed after the eruption of TNV movement in Tripura, and the entire nation was shocked, Rev. Dr. Rieveh Cunville, an American Church leader and a director of the Bible Society of India, was happy. It was a "nationalist uprising" according to him and he hoped this political upheaval would make the tribals more receptive to the Gospel.[58] Cunville hailed tribal assertion for rights and freedom like those of Mizoram, Nagaland and Meghalaya and observed that if large numbers are to come to Christ *via* these peoples movement, the Tripura Baptist Christian Union (TBCU) would require aid from other Churches and Missions. The Union continues to describe Hinduism as a threat to the tribal identity.[59] These facts support the statement of a Naga University Teacher that "Christianity along with English education have played a very significant role in the Naga society in their struggle for a sovereign and independent Nagalim.[60]

The spread of Christianity was at faster rate after Independence. The conversions were driven by the fact that the political and bureaucratic leadership was mostly in the hands of the educated Christians. Even theology students received scholarships in the state. Being Christian conferred social status and tangible rewards including education and the jobs.

REFERENCES

1. Sema, Hokise, Emergence of Nagaland, p. 51
2. Bareh, H., *Nagaland District Gazetteer, Kohima distict,* p. 92.
3. *Ibid.,* p. 93.
4. Alemchiba, M., *A Brief Historical Account of Nagaland,* pp. 134-35.
5. Puthenpurakal, Joseph, Dr., *Baptist Mission in Nagaland,* p. 106.
6. Ao Naga Baptist Church Centenary Album, Impur (1972), Preface, p. 2.
7. Puthenpurakal, *op. cit.,* p. 114.
8. Prakash Singh, *Nagaland,* NBT, New Delhi, 1995, pp. 171-72.
9. *Ibid.,* p. 170.
10. Census of India, 1891.
11. Kumer, Dr.B.B., *Tribal Societies of India,* p. 234.
12. Johnstone, J., *Importance of Education,*in Verrier Elwin's *Nagas in the Nineteenth Century,* pp. 598-999.
13. Alemchiba, *op. cit.,* p. 153.
14. *Ibid.*
15. *Ibid.,* p. 154.
16. Elwin, *op. cit.,* p. 513.
17. *Ibid.,* p. 515.

18. *Ibid.*, p. 598.
19. Millls, J.P., *The Lotha Nagas,* pp. XI-XII.
20. Puthenpurakal, *op.cit.*, pp. 140-45.
21. *Ibid.*, pp. 146-49.
22. Mills, J.P., *The Ao Nagas*, p. 412.
23. *Ibid.*
24. *Ibid.*, pp. 411-12.
25. *Ibid.*, p. 413, n. 3.
26. *Ibid.*, p. 414.
27. Horam, Dr. M., *Social Change in Nagaland,* in *The North Eastern Research Bulletin,* Vol. 6, Dibrugarh,1975, p. 14.
28. Shishak, T.A., *Higher Education in Nagaland* Unpublished Ph. D. Thesis, p. 66.
29. Hutton, J.H., *The Angami Nagas,* p. 180.
30. Centenary Aibum, *op. cit,* preface; p. 1.
31. Puthenpurakal, *op. cit.*, p. 153.
32. *Ibid.*
33. *Ibid.*
34. *Ibid.*
35. *Ibid.*, p. 154.
36. Mills, *The Ao Nagas,* p. 412.
37. *Ibid.*, p. 421.
38. *Ibid.*
39. Puthenpurakal, p. 110.
40. *Ibid.*
41. *Ibid.*
42. *Ibid.*
43. *Ibid.*, p. 152.
44. Horam, *op. cit.*, p. 14.
45. Mills, *The Ao Nagas,* p. 418.
46. Haimendorf, C. Von, Furer, *The Naked Nagas,* pp. 51-55.
47. Horam, *op. cit.*
48. Hokise Sema, *op. cit.*, p. 52.
49. *Ibid.*, p. 53.
50. Ganguli, Milada, *Pilgrimage to the Nagas,* p. 193.
51. Mills, *The Ao Nagas,* pp. 414-15.
52. *Ibid.*, p. 415.
53. *Ibid.*
54. *Ibid.*
55. Kumar, *op. cit.*, pp. 244-45.
56. Prakash Singh, *op. cit.*, p. 173.
57. Tehelka, Special Report, 10 July 2004.
58. Rabijit Chaudhury, *Religious Undertones in Ethnic Issues in North-East, in Administrator,* Vol. XXXIX, No. 4, p. 27.
59. *Ibid.*
60. Proceedings of the Seminar on *"Foundations of Naga Peoplehood: Road Maps"*, Kohima, Centre for Democracy and Tribal Studies, 11 April, 2003, p. 26; Paper by Dr. Xavier P. Mao on "Nagalim and Naga Nationalism."

13

THE NAGA AUTONOMY MOVEMENT

The Naga Club, set up in 1918 by the British administration at Kohima, was the first organization of its kind in the Naga inhabited area. The Lotha and Ao Tribal Councils were formed in 1923 and 1928 respectively. The Naga Hills District Tribal Council was established in 1945 on the nucleus of the Naga Club. Its aim was to work for rehabilitation and reconstruction of war devastated areas of Naga Hills. C.R. Pawsey, the Deputy Commissioner of Naga Hills district, was instrumental in its establishment. The nomenclature of the Council was changed to Naga National Council (NNC) at its Wokha meeting held in April 1946. It had 29 members. The organization did not have representatives from all the tribes. These organizations were politicized soon after their establishment.

Simon Commission Memorandum

The Naga Club presented a Memorandum to the Simon Commission in 1929 praying for keeping the Hills beyond the ambit of proposed reforms and to place them directly under the British Government. Their apprehension that the "introduction of foreign laws and customs" may supersede their "own customary laws" and the desire to be left alone to determine for themselves "as in ancient times" was expressed in the memorandum. It said:

> "If the British Government, however, wants to throw us away, we pray that we should not be thrust to the mercy of the (Indian) people who could never have conquered us themselves, and to whom we were never subjected but leave us alone to determine for ourselves as in ancient times."

It needs mention here that the Naga Club was set up by the British administration. Its members were on the pay role of the Government. Among the twenty signatories the memorandum submitted to the Simon Commission, there were 14 Angamis (one Head interpreter, three interpreters, one Peshkar, one doctor, one Potdar, three masters, one treasurer, one sub-overseer, one chaprasi and one clerk) and two Kacha Nagas (one interpreter and the other clerk). There were four interpreters one each from Sema, Lotha, Rengma and Kuki tribes. There was none from Ao, Sangtam, Chang, Phom, Konyak, Khiamngan and other tribes among the signatories.

Some of the points raised in the said memorandum provide interesting reading and reflect the colonial mindset and perception of the British Deputy Commissioner stationed at Kohima. He was working behind the curtain and was the friend, philosopher and the guide of the staff working under him. Strangely, the signatories had nothing against the continuing British rule; they wrote: "...but as the administration of our Hills continued to be in the hands of the British officers, we did not consider it necessary to raise any protest in the past."[1]

They further wrote: "Before the British Government conquered our country in 1879-80, we were living in a state of intermittent warfare with the Assamese of the Assam valley to the North and West of our country and Manipuris in the South. They never conquered us nor were we subjected to their rule. On the other hand, we were always a terror to these people." The memorandum highlighted the situation and wrote: "Our country within the administered area consists of more than eight Tribes, quite different from one another with quite different languages which cannot be understood by each other, and there are more tribes outside the administered area which are not known at present. We have no Unity among us and it is really the British Government that is holding us together now." The memorandum talked about poor education scenario, numerical inferiority, difference between the languages and lack of social affinity between the Nagas and the plainsmen. It wrote: Our language is quite different from those of the plains and we have no social affinities with Hindus or Muslims. We are looked down upon by the one for our 'beef' and the other for our 'pork' and by both for our want in Education which is not due to any fault of ours."[2]

It was feared that their placement under the reformed scheme might lead to sale of their lands to enable them to meet the requirement of heavy taxation.[3]

The memorandum carries much imaginary myth about the Nagas and their neighbours. It was because the brain of the British Deputy Commissioner was responsible for the whole exercise preparing mindset for British Protectorate which culminated in Coupland Proposal for separating tribes as protectorate of British Crown after 1947. Both history and tradition link Nagas with the Assamese and the Manipuris. There are numerous Naga legends of their common origin.[4] The Kacharis allow the Nagas in their houses considering them to be their brothers, but not the Kukis. There are instance of Lothas fighting the war against the Burmese with the Assamese. Ahom-Naga relations cannot be explained in isolationist frame. Gait has mentioned that the Patkai was fixed as the Boundary of the Ahom kingdom in a formal treaty in 1401.[5]

Naga National Council: The Initial Stand

The Wokha Conference of the Naga National Council drafted a 4-point memorandum on 19 June, 1945 about the future of the Nagas to be submitted to His Majesty's Government. The resolutions of the said memorandum, approved by its general body, were as given below:

1. The Naga National Council stands for the solidarity of the Naga tribes, including those of the unadministered areas;
2. The Council strongly protests against the grouping of Assam with Bengal;
3. The Naga Hills should be constitutionally included in an autonomous Assam in a free India with local autonomy and duly safeguarded for the interests of the Nagas; and
4. The Naga tribes should have a separate electorate.

Naga National Council: The About-turn

The above-mentioned resolutions of the Naga National Council clearly indicated that the NNC wanted the Nagas to remain in free India as a part of Assam. But the NNC lacked consistency. It very soon changed its stand. The idea of self-determination was an afterthought, which was voiced in the NNC's resolution drafted on 10 February, 1947 to be submitted to His Majesty's Government and the Government of India. It demanded self-determination for the Nagas and for setting up of Interim Government for ten years, at the end of which the Nagas would be free to decide the form of the government of their liking. The memorandum sent by the NNC to His Majesty's Government, accordingly incorporated these resolutions. The memorandum further said that a constitution drawn up by the people not knowing the Nagas would be 'unsuitable' and 'unacceptable' to them. The Naga Nationalist Council leaders insisted that Gopi Nath Bordoloi Sub-Committee should accept the points raised in their memorandum and incorporate them in the report to be submitted to the Constituent Assembly of India. The Bordoloi Sub-Committee did not accept their demands. The Sub-Committee's suggestions were, however, incorporated in the Sixth Schedule in Article 244 of the Constitution, which provided for the formation of the District Councils in the Hill districts of Assam. This provision was not accepted by the NNC and the District Council was not formed in the Naga Hills district.

Phizo replaced the moderate leadership of the NNC just before Independence. The moderate voice of "Nagas under autonomous Assam in free India" was never heard again from the NNC platform, except for a brief period, after that. The demand of the right of self-determination voiced under his leadership was based on the following:

(*i*) Ethnic distinctiveness.

(*ii*) Distinct social life, way of living, laws and customs, etc.

(*iii*) Different religion – Animism and Christianity.

Another memorandum was submitted by the NNC on 19 May, 1947, in which it was clarified that the 10-year Interim Government might be a government of the Naga people with full powers over legislative, executive and judicial matters, and that the Guardian power might maintain such force in the Hills as was considered essential for its defence. The Gopi Nath Bordoloi Committee visited Kohima on 20 May, 1947 and had series of talks with NNC leaders. The talks did not yield anything.

Sir Akbar Hydari, the Governor of Assam was the next visitor, who came to Kohima on 26 June, 1947. He had meeting with the Naga leaders on 27, 28 and 29 June, 1947. They arrived at a 9-point Understanding.[6] It provided for the basic safeguards for Naga culture and way of life. The Nagas were assured about the preservation of their customary laws and rights over their lands and resources. The 9-point Understanding recognised the right of the Nagas to develop themselves according to their expressed wishes. It postulated that no laws passed by the Provincial or Central Legislature effecting its terms or the religious practices of the Nagas shall have legal force in the Naga Hills without the consent of the Naga Council. The Naga Council was to control for whatever it was prepared to pay in the executive matters. All civil or criminal cases were to be disposed off by dully-constituted Naga Courts according to the Naga Customary Laws. Imposition, collection and expenditure of the land revenue and house tax were to be the responsibility of the Naga Council. It was agreed that the land would not be alienated to a non-Naga without the consent of the Naga Council. Controversy arose about the interpretation of the Article 9 of the Understanding, which read:

> "The Governor of Assam as the agent of the Government of the Indian Union will have a special responsibility for a period of 10 years to ensure the due observance of this agreement; at the end of this period the Naga Council will be asked whether they require the above agreement to be extended for a further period or a new agreement regarding the future of the Naga people arrived at."

The difference in the interpretation of the last article created misunderstanding. The Council interpreted the last point to mean that they may have right to opt out of India after ten years. The official interpretation was to mean more acceptable arrangements for the smooth functioning of autonomy. It resulted into disagreement and Hydari agreement broke down. The very existence of Hydari agreement was forgotten very soon. Many deny even its very existence. But it continued to have publicity value for the NNC. While creating controversy about the interpretation of Article 9 of the said agreement it did not care to remember that a person holding such a high post (of Governor) was never to forget his brief and cross his limits. After all how a Governor can initiate a process having the grave implication of the dismemberment of a country. The NNC interpretation was obviously self-serving without relevance to the realities.

A copy of the said Understanding was sent by Governor Hydari to Pt. Jawaharlal Nehru on 7 July, 1947. He forwarded the same to the Constituent Assembly on 12 July, 1947. The Governor's copy of the document had the expression 'Naga Council', whereas the document circulated by NNC used the expression 'Naga National Council'. The official document was called 'Heads of Proposed Understanding'; in NNC document, it was called 'Heads of Proposed Agreement'. The interpolation of the word 'National' and the use of 'agreement', rather than 'understanding' were obviously done to build up the image of NNC and Phizo.[7]

A.Z. Phizo led a series of delegations to Delhi to press for the sovereignty demand of Nagaland. He met Mahatma Gandhi once and Nehru several times. Nehru and U Nu, the Prime Minister of Burma visited Kohima in March 1953. The Naga leaders wanted to submit a memorandum to the Prime Minister, which was not allowed. This led to walk-out by the Nagas of the meeting organized to welcome the two Prime Ministers. Nehru was mortified. President Rajendra Prasad and Congress President Dhebar Bhai refused to meet them after that incident.

Phizo declared Nagaland's Independence on 14 August, 1947, a day earlier than that of India. The Nagas of the Naga Hills district did not participate in District Council formation. They boycotted 1952 general elections. Phizo conducted a plebiscite during May to August 1951 in which 99 per cent Nagas are said to have voted for the Naga Independence. These steps boosted the morale of secessionists and highly demoralized the administration.

Certain facts regarding the plebiscite conducted by Phizo and highly publicized by the secessionists are rarely talked about and heard. These are:

(*i*) The plebiscite was not properly and fairly conducted. The boxes for receiving 'yes' and 'no' votes were kept in separate rooms. In no way the identity of the persons casting negative votes was to remain secret. The people did not, therefore, dare to vote for 'no'.

(*ii*) The plebiscite was conducted in the limited area of Kohima and Mokokchung only.

(*iii*) The results were inflated.

The NNC was the only political forum of all shades of Naga public opinion before it went into the total control of Phizo. Young educated people continued and still continue to be a force in the politics of the Hills of North-East India, and Naga Hills and Tuensang were no exceptions. Most of the educated people were moderates, but they used to leave the platform for government jobs and failed to register their prolonged presence and to guide the opinion. The bureaucratic shortsighted decision of the Assam Government debarring Government servants from becoming members of the NNC further weakened the position of the moderates. This was a counter-productive step where most of the intelligentsia were Government servants.

In spite of the above factors, the power struggle continued within NNC between the moderates led by T. Aliba Imti and the separatists led by Phizo. It culminated in Phizo's resignation from the NNC in 1949. He, however, joined it again and became its president in December 1950. This, he could accomplish by a series of shrewd moves; but his victory was possible with only one vote.[8]

T. Aliba Imti, the then Joint Secretary of the Tribal Council has mentioned about certain questions often discussed among the members without unanimous answers.[9]

- What are Nagas going to do after the British left India?
- What is the future of the Nagas?
- Are we Indians?
- Are not we a part of India? What will be our future provisions?
- What are our safeguards?
- Where do we stand in the future?

The opinions differed. "Some favoured independence, others an autonomous status in free India, while yet others desired protectorate status under the British Government for a specified period of time."[10]

The moderate voice was never heard from the platform of the NNC after the organization going in the full control of the Phizo and his followers. But there was never any such period when the moderate voice was not heard in Nagaland. The Reforming Committee of the Naga National Council, the three Naga People's Conventions and the Naga People's Organization (the party which won 1964 Nagaland Legislative Assembly elections) etc. remained always in moderate hands.

The Phizo and his followers started civil disobedience movement soon after. The activities, started by them, among others, included: (*a*) non-payment of house-tax; (*b*) non-co-operation with the government in its development schemes; (*c*) refusal to supply labour and food-items to touring officers; (*d*) boycott of national and official celebrations; (*e*) return of red blankets—the badges of their authority—by the Gaon-Burras to the Deputy Commissioner; (*f*) forced resignation of the school teachers; and (*g*) forced withdrawal of the students from schools. A point needs special mention here that the top underground leaders sent their own children for higher education, but prevented poor Nagas from sending their children even to the village schools. Backward tribes and those living in the small villages were the worst sufferers. Rich Nagas sent their children to Shillong, Darjeeling and elsewhere for schooling and higher education that poor people could hardly afford to do. Their children were forcibly recruited in Naga Army and they silently suffered. Schools thrived in Shillong from Nagaland's money.

As proclaimed by Phizo, the movement remained non-violent in the beginning. But it could not remain so and very soon, in early 1950s, violent clashes started taking place. The climax reached in 1956.

The underground slowly spread their activities in Tuensang also. In fact Tuensang saw the simultaneous growth of administration and underground activities in early fifties. The attempts to recruit young men in the armed underground ranks resulted into the mobilisation of an army of 500 men by the end of 1955. Their number further increased soon after. The government recruited armed village guards. Murder, arson, loot and intimidation of moderates and government servants continued unabated. The village guards and Assam police failed to control the situation. Army was called in the hills in 1956. The Naga Hills Disturbed Area Ordinance and Assam Maintenance of Public Order were promulgated in Naga Hills. After replacement of Assam Police Battalions by Indian Armed Forces, Special Powers Act was also enforced. A period of intense violent opposition started. The rebels operated in the cover of dense forests. It was a new experience for the army men to fight a guerilla battle in an area devoid of communications. Most of the army battalions were new to the scene while the rebels knew every inch of it.

The Chief of the Army Staff issued official instructions in 1955, according to which military operations were not to be conducted on war footing. The instruction issued was the following:

> "You must remember that all the people of the area in which you are operating are fellow-Indians. They may have a different religion, they may pursue a different way of life, but they are Indians, and the very fact that they are different and yet part of India is a reflection of India's greatness. Some of these people are misguided and have taken to arms against their own people, and are disrupting the peace of this area. You are to protect the mass of the people from these disruptive elements. You are not there to fight the people in the area, but to protect them. You are fighting only those who threaten the people and who are a danger to the lives and properties of the people. You must, therefore, do everything possible to win their confidence and respect and to help them feel that they belong to India."[11]

Malicious Propaganda

Phizo, at one place, asked the villagers "if they wanted their lands to remain with them or were willing to surrender them to India."[12] He raised the issue of colour also and opined that the Nagas favoured white people, working as missionaries and administrators among them for many years than black people of the plains.[13] Propaganda, that Nagas may be converted to Hinduism; may be prevented from taking beef, were believed by simple, uneducated Nagas, most of whom hardly knew the people of rest of India. The malicious, baseless propaganda and raising emotive issues by the Phizoites were never countered by the Assam and Central Government. The Naga people became highly suspicious; started fearing India. The Secessionist benefited.

The Army was working under very trying conditions, but with considerable restraint. The situation was highly abnormal and the use of the army was inevitable. It, however, cannot be denied that Army is a crude instrument for handling intra-country crisis like this and none can deny that some excess were not committed. The underground repeatedly accused the Army of having committed 'atrocities' and attempted genocide in Nagaland. Their charges were highly exaggerated and even Naga leaders did not like the same. Keneth Kerhuo, the then Field Director of the Angami Baptist Mission, said:

> "Owing to the violent activities of the Naga Home Guards, most of the Churches stopped functioning in Naga Hills sometime ago. The villages were so terror-stricken that they could not even enter their own homes. How could they come to the Churches?
>
> Thanks to the Army, confidence has returned to the villages, and the peaceful Nagas are able to look after their affairs unafraid. The Churches are having regular service attended by bigger congregations than ever. Quite a number of Army Officers and men are Christians. They make it a point to attend Church services. I have heard nothing but the highest praise of Army Officers and men in general from several Nagas of different tribes. They all say the way Army personnel rehabilitate villages and bring medical succour to the sick and the infirm shows that they literally implement the following words of the Lord: 'Love your enemies, do good to them that hate you, bless them that curse you, pray for them that despitefully use you."[14]

A group of Nagas, including J.B. Jasokie, Keneth Kerhuo, Ruzhukhrie Sekhose, Khiya, (Mrs.) Luci Dino, (Mrs.) Dzobvunno and (Miss) Kerino Zinyu, protested over the charge of immorality against the Security Forces personnel and issued their statement:

> "We are shocked to hear that the Nagas who are at present engaged in violent activities in Nagas Hills, in their zeal to

vilify officers and men of the Armed Forces, speak light-heartedly of Naga women-folk and even describe their own daughters, sisters and wives as harlots and prostitutes. To say the least, these Nagas who speak so irreverently of Naga girls, have lost all sense of proportion as also sense of shame. We who are intimately connected with the Angami area and are engaged in social or religious uplift work, can say that the Armed Forces personnel in our area have behaved in the most exemplary manner possible. On several occasions they have praised the modesty of the Naga girls. No Armed Force in the world could have behaved better than the Indian Armed Forces have done in Naga Hills."[15]

In March 1956, the insurgents formed the Federal Government of Nagaland. They also framed their constitution, which runs as follows:

"Nagalnd is a people's sovereign republic. This has been so from time immemorial. There will be a parliament with 100 *tatars* (M.Ps.), the president will be elected by the people and his cabinet will consist of 15 *Kilonsers* (Ministers)."
"Nagaland will maintain permanent military neutrality. There will be no standing army for the maintenance of law and order. There will be a department of Home Guards headed by a Chief to function in a dual capacity of police and patriot soldier."

They further declared:

"Land belongs to the people and it will remain so. There will be no land tax, and other forms of taxation will be formulated by different administrative units."
"All forms of trade, business, industry, transport and other public utility will be free and will be in the hands of the people."
"Religion will be free."
"Each Naga village is a republic in its own right. Each Naga family or tribe occupies its own distinct region, and shall continue as before to exercise full authority over its own affairs, including land, community organization, social and religious practices and customs."

"Men and women above 22 years of age will have equal rights of voting."

There will be equal wages for "equal work irrespective of sex."

There was provision for the appointment of *Angs* (*i.e.* Governors), Advisers, Deputy Commissioners, Magistrates, Ambassadors, Judges etc. in underground set-up. They had a Commander-in-Chief of the military organization of Home Guards, and men of all other ranks. The arms and ammunitions consisted of those left behind in Second World War and arms and ammunitions captured in raids and seized from individuals.

They also established an underground Federal High Court.

Phizo also organized Naga Youth Movement (NYM) and Naga Women's Society (NWS). NYM members acted as couriers, raised subscriptions, constructed camps, and collected information about the movement and deployment of Security Forces. The volunteers of NWS worked as cooks and nurses, tailored the uniforms and looked after their recreation.

The innocent villagers were the worst sufferers in the conflict. Dissentions stated surfacing soon in the ranks and files of the underground. T. Sakhrie and some others resigned from the N.N.C. Shakhrie, who was highly intelligent and who very brilliantly handled the publicity drive of the NNC, understood the futility of the entire exercise. After his parting of ways from Phizo, Shakhrie was abducted one night, taken to the jungle tortured and cruelly murdered in January 1956. The next important person to pay the price for the parting of ways and differences of opinion were Dr. Imkongliba Ao and Kaito Sema. Attempts on the life of many, such as Jasokie and Hokishe Sema, were made repeatedly.

The efforts started afresh to end the state of belligerence. People disliked violence and conflict and they took courage and started mobilising public opinion in favour of peaceful settlement of the problem. A Naga Peace Organizing Committee was formed in early 1956 with Levi as Chairman and Jasokie as Joint Secretary. The objects of the Committee were: (1) to establish peace and tranquility throughout the Naga area, (2) to redeem the innocent Naga Public from falling victims to the atmosphere of turmoil, and (3) to persuade the hostile Nagas to desist from violent activities. The Committee, in a resolution passed on 24 March, 1956, regretted "the people being carried away by the tidal wave of mistaken exuberance." Its opinion was that the violent activities were against the best interests of the Naga people and that these would bring them immense suffering.[16]

In the meantime, 1957 general elections were held and three Nagas—Khelhose Sema, Chubatemsu Ao and Subedar Satsuo Angami—filed nominations and got elected as MLAs of Assam Assembly unopposed. Mr. Khelhose was appointed Deputy Minister. All of them resigned on 1st December 1957, when a separate unit—Naga Hills Tuensang Area was formed.

First Naga People's Convention

An All Tribes Naga People's Convention was convened from 22nd to 26th August, 1957, under the chairmanship of Dr. Imkongliba Ao, J.B. Jasokie was its secretary. 1760 delegates and over 2000 visitors from every Naga tribe attended it. The convention denounced violence and advocated settlement of Naga problem through negotiation. The underground Nagas did not join the convention. The demand for independence was formally given up and the following main demands were made:

(*a*) Creation of single administrative unit comprising of Naga Hills district of Assam and Tuensang Frontier Division of NEFA.

(*b*) Restoration of the reserved forests carved out of the Naga Hills district in 1921.

(*c*) Declaration of general amnesty.

(*d*) Certain administrative changes as interim measure.

A nine member delegation of the Naga People's Convention under the leadership of Dr. Imkongliba Ao met the Governor at Shillong and the Prime Minister in New Delhi to present their resolutions soon after the convention.

Formation of Naga Hills Tuensang Area

Nehru was sympathetic to their demands and conceded their main demands; the Naga Hills Tuensang Area (NHTA) came into being on 1st August, 1957. The Assam Government granted general amnesty. It is worth-noting that the Nagas of Manipur in a largely attended meeting under the chairmanship of Mr. Anal, a prominent Congress leader passed a resolution to merge Naga areas of Manipur also in the new political setup.

Naga Hills Tuensang Area was formed basing on the Naga Hills Tuensang Area (Administrative) Regulations, 1957 promulgated by the President of India in exercise of the powers conferred by Article 240 of the Constitution read with sub-paragraph (2) of paragraph 18 of the Sixth Schedule to the Constitution.

Some important articles of the regulation are reproduced below:

> "The Naga Hills-Tuensang Area shall be divided into three districts to be called Kohima District, Mokokchung District and Tuensang District, each comprising the areas respectively set out against it in the Schedule."
>
> "The administration of Naga Hills Tuensang Area shall be carried on by the Governor of Assam as the agent of the President."
>
> "The Central Government may appoint a Commissioner for the Naga Hills Tuensang Area to assist the Governor of Assam; and the Governor may appoint a Deputy Commissioner for each of the districts therein and the Deputy Commissioners shall perform their functions under the supervision and control of the Commissioner."

The existing provisions of law and taxation were to continue in the NHTA till modifications were made by competent authority.

The Second and Third Naga People's Conventions

The Second Naga People's Convention was held in Ungma village in Mokokchung district in May 1958. There were protests and threats from the underground. A Liaison Committee was appointed to contact the underground people, but there was no response from their side. Ultimately, the convention appointed a Drafting Committee to formulate their demands. The Drafting Committee prepared a sixteen point memorandum (attached *vide* Annexure III) for the constitution of a separate state within Indian Union. The Third Naga

People's Convention was held in Mokokchung from 22nd to 26th October 1959. It approved the draft of the sixteen-point memorandum.

The Naga People's Convention delegates met the Governor of Assam at Shillong in April 1960 for preliminary discussion. This was followed by a meeting of 15 members and four consultants representing all the Naga tribes, with the Prime Minister in July 1960. Some of the delegates were Jasokie Angami, Chubatoshi Jamir, Chiten Jamir, Khelhose Sema, T.N. Angami, P. Demo and Thanwang Konyak. The four consultants were Shilu Ao, H. Zopianga, Sashimeren Aier and Goyiopra. The consultants were in Government service. The Prime Minister accepted their demands in principle. Their main demand was the establishment of Nagaland state. The Prime Minister announced the result of these discussions in the Lok Sabha on 1 August, 1960:

> "A new State to be called 'Nagaland' will be established within the Indian Union comprising the territory of the existing Naga Hills and the Tuensang Area. The same person will be appointed as the Governor of Assam and the Governor of Nagaland and the existing jurisdiction of the Assam High Court over the area comprising the new State would continue. There will be a transitional period during which an interim body will be constituted with representatives from every Naga tribe to assist and advise the Governor in the administration of Nagaland. The Governor will have special responsibility for law and order during this transitional period and for so long as the law and order situation continues to remain disturbed on account of hostile activities. Since the financial resources of the new State will be extremely limited, and large grants from the Central Government may be necessary not only for the development schemes, but also to maintain the efficiency of the administration, the Governor will have general responsibility for ensuring that the funds made available by the Government of India are expended for the purposes for which they are approved by the Central Government.
>
> There will be a Legislative Assembly to which the Council of Ministers of the new State will be responsible.

Certain safeguards, as in the existing Sixth Schedule of the Constitution, will be provided for the religious and social practices of the Nagas, Naga customary laws and procedure and the ownership and transfer of land. Otherwise the existing laws relating to the administration of the civil and criminal justice will continue to remain in force. Jurisdiction of the High Court of Assam will also continue. Special provision will be made for the administration of the Tuensang district in accordance with the wishes of the people inhabiting that district. There are some other matters of relatively lesser importance on which also full understanding has been reached between the Government of India and the Naga leaders. It is hoped, therefore, that there will be no room for any misunderstanding in future about the Government of India's intention and what they propose to do to implement the understanding reached during the recent discussions. It is now the intention of the Government of India to give effect to the arrangements reached with the Naga leaders without delay. This will involve amendment of the Constitution and a bill will be placed before Parliament for approval in due course.

"I take this opportunity to express our satisfaction at the agreement reached with the Naga leaders. We have always regarded the Nagas as full Indian citizens. I have said to the Naga people several times in the past that there could be no question of independence for the Nagas. India achieved her independence thirteen years ago and the Nagas are as independent as other Indian citizens. We have not the slightest desire to interfere in the tribal customs and usage of the Nagas or in their distinctive way of life. The Nagas have been anxious to have separate State within the Indian Union. The agreement now reached with them should enable them to find the fullest opportunity of self-expression and we sincerely hope that the new agreement will result in the rapid restoration of normal conditions in the area. I must, however, make it clear that no Government can permit hostile activities on its soil, and while we are ready to give our fullest support to those who will co-operate in giving effect to the agreement just reached, we shall continue to deal firmly with the hostile elements. This is an unpleasant but necessary task and I trust that the Naga leaders will co-operate fully in putting an end to the disloyal activities of a minority of their people."

Formation of Interim Body

As per the provisions of the Nagaland (Transitional Provision) Regulation, 1961 (No. 2 of 1961), the Interim Body was formed for three years with 45 members representing all the tribes of Nagaland. It started functioning *w.e.f.* 18 February, 1961. The Interim Body elected five-member Executive Council consisting of P. Shilu Ao as Chief Executive Councillor. Hokishe Sema, J.B. Jasokie, R.C. Chiten Jamir and Akum Imlong were Executive Councillors. Dr. Imkongliba Ao took most prominent part in the Naga People's Convention activities. He was elected the chairman. The Interim Body had strange combination of old and the young, experienced and unexperienced, government servants and the ex-undergrounds. Shilu Ao, Hokishe Sema and M. Kithan were ex-government servants; Jasokie and Julekhemba Ao were ex-underground, and Levi, retired head clerk of the Deputy Commissioner's office, was also an ex-government servant.

The underground did not approve the activities of the Naga People's Convention. They disliked the formation of Interim Body and the Exective Council. The members of these bodies were threatened and condemned. The words like 'trators' and 'stooges' were used for them. Dr. Imkongliba Ao, the architect of the negotiations and peaceful settlement, was assassinated, just after few months, in his home-town, Mokokchung. The Interim Body elected T.N. Angami as its new Chairman, and M. Kithan as Deputy Chairman.

Formation of the Nagaland State

The Parliament passed the Constitution (Thirteenth) Amendment Act in September 1962 to provide for the formation of Nagaland as the 16th state of the Indian Republic. The State of Nagaland Act, 1962 provided constitutional and legal framework for the new state. The President, Dr. S. Radhakrishnan, inaugurated the state on 1st December, 1963. The Interim Body and the Executive Council started functioning as the Nagaland Legislative Assembly and the Nagaland Cabinet and the Chairman of the Interim Body as the Speaker.

Elections for the Nagaland Legislative Assembly were held in early 1964. The people of Kohima and Mokokchung elected 40 members; six members were nominated by the Tuensang Regional Council. People elected Nagaland Nationalist Organization party to power. The Minister-Incharge of Tuensang Affairs was chosen from among the nominated members of that district. Tuensang Regional Council nominated twelve member for the next Assembly. There was provision for the nomination from Tuensang for ten years only. The people elected a 60-member Assembly after that period.

REFERENCES

1. Copy of the Memorandum submitted to the Simon Commission is attached *vide* Annexure I.
2. Plese see Annexue I.
3. *Ibid.*
4. See *The Angami Nagas* by J.H. Hutton, pp. 260, 345; *The Lotha Nagas* by J.P. Mills, p. 3.
5. Gait, Sir Edward, *The History of Assam,* pp. 79-81.
6. Copy attached *vide* Annexure II.
7. Prakash Singh, *Nagaland,* p. 81, note 1.
8. Pillai, Lt. Gen. (Retd.), Sushil K. *Anatomy of an Insurgency: Ethnicity and Identity in Nagaland,* in Faultline, Vol. 3; p. 51.
9. *Ibid.*, p. 49; cited from Imti Aliba's *Reminiscence: Impur to NNC* (1988).
10. S.K. Pillai, *op. cit.*, p. 49.
11. B.B. Kumar, *Re-Organization of North-East India,* p. 29.
12. Prakash Singh, *op. cit.*, p. 84.
13. Lt. Gen. (Retd.) S. K. Pillai, *op. cit.*, p. 50.
14. *Naga Khabar,* Vol. 1, No. 6.; quoted by Prakash Singh, *op. cit.*, p. 89.
15. *Ibid.*, No, 7; quoted as above.
16. Prakash Singh, *op. cit.*, p. 91.

14

MYTHS, MISINFORMATIONS AND THE PROPAGANDA

The role of the myths, misinformations and the propaganda in support of the on-going strife in Nagaland have never been studied properly for its historical authenticity. Some of these are carried due to ignorance; others knowingly. Even highly educated persons talk on these issues without caring to confirm the facts. Myth-making and misinformation campaigns downgrade the level of academic debate to that of sloganeering and propaganda. It is interesting to analyse some of these made from time to time.

Phizo, while touring in the Naga Hills, asked in a particular village, whether they (the villagers) wanted their lands to remain with them or were willing to surrender them to India?[1] He gave another similar statement, which said:

> "The white Government has gone, a black Government has come. This Government will take away your land; they will tax your houses, your cows; your pigs will be counted and you will be asked to pay according to the number of pigs you keep. You will not be allowed to drink. Do you want such a Government or Independence? If you are independent you will enjoy life as we had before the British came."[2]

These statements need no elaboration. Its motive and impact on simple, unsophisticated, uneducated Nagas is self-evident. It was intended to create fear-psychosis and to heighten the suspicion of the Nagas for the outsiders. It was given as a part of his strategy to win over the Nagas for secession from India. He makes the statement emotive by bringing the context of white and black. He forgets that many Naga tribes are black in colour.[3] Practically, everything in Phizo's statements operates at the level of propaganda. But, Phizo, and his organization, Naga National Council, was not the first to indulge in such statement making. Oft-quoted Simon Commission Memorandum, submitted by a section of the Naga and Kuki employees of the Deputy Commissioner's office of Kohima on 10 January, 1929, is the first document using such oversimplified statements, as we find in that of Phizo. Many myths crystallized in the British colonial thinking find their expression in that document as well as in Phizo's statements. Both are devoid of historical basis. Phizo is not the originator; he simply echoes the former.

Myth of Naga Freedom

According to the Memorandum submitted to the Simon Commission, the Nagas were not subjected to the rule of the Assamese and the Manipuris. It stated:

> "Before the British Government conquered our country in 1879-1880, we were living in a state of intermittent warfare with the Assamese of the Assam Valley to the North and West of our country and Manipuris in the South. They never conquered us nor were we subjected to their rule."[4]

The statement is factually erroneous and historically incorrect. The truth is that the Nagas were not only subjected to the rule of the (*a*) Assamese/Ahoms and (*b*) Manipuris, but also that of the (*c*) Kacharis and (*d*) the Singphos. According to Woodthorpe, the Assam Rajahs held sway over these hills and they exacted tribute from the Nagas.[5] Gait also held the similar view that the Nagas paid annual tribute to the Ahom kings.[6] It is significant and needs mention that Patkai, on the Indo-Myanmar border, was fixed as the boundary of the Ahom kingdom of Assam, according to a treaty concluded in 1401.[7]

The boundary between the Manipur and the Angami area was settled before the British occupation of the Naga Hills districts. Thus the Manipuri Kings also ruled over the Nagas before the British conquered the Nagas Hills. The Nagas of North Cachar Hills were ruled by the Kachari Kings before the British arrived in the North-East. The Singphos ruled over the Eastern Nagas.

The Myth of Naga Terror

The Simon Commission Memorandum further says that the Nagas were always a terror to the Assamese and the Manipuris. It is again a baseless statement, not corroborated by history. The truth is that the history of Assam, as well as that of Manipur records very few cases of Naga raids. Mills has written about the relationship of the Ahoms with the Ao Nagas (who are one of the most educated, most developed and most important tribes of Nagaland) thus: "For as far back as they can remember the Aos have been friendly with the rulers of Assam and the plains have never been used as a happy hunting-ground for head-seekers."[8] He further writes: "For long the Aos had maintained friendly relations with the Ahom Rajas, and several villages received grants of land in the plains in exchange for presents and promises to refrain from raiding."[9] Thus, as the history attests, the Nagas were never a terror for the Ahoms and the Assamese. The same is true about the history of Manipur. Rather, the Nagas had cordial relationship with them and helped them during the days of their distress, such as during the Burmese invasions. Gait, in his *History of Assam* has mentioned about very few cases of Naga raids during the Ahom rule. In every such time the Ahoms sent punitive expeditions and brought the situation under control.[10] Thus the views expressed in the said memorandum were based on the back projection of the Naga history of the early British Period and on the Britisher's own experience of the Naga turbulence. It needs mention that the British, experienced only the turbulent behaviour of the Nagas. The Naga raids increased considerably only during the early British rule, which made them obsessed. The British had to keep guards to protect Amguri Tea Estate from the head-hunting raids of even the Ao Nagas, who never indulged in such raids during the Ahom days, and who, like other Nagas, were never a terror for the Ahoms.

The Myth of Exploitation

There is nothing to show that the Nagas did ever experience economic exploitation by their neighbours. Similarly, there was neither any attempt any time to interfere with their religious practices, nor was any attempt to change their social structure. It is a historic fact that a King of Assam/an Ahom King, sent even his wife to a Naga village. Beef and Pork used to be taboos even among some Naga tribes [11] and there are many Hindu communities eating beef and pork in India. [12] The statements "We are looked down upon by the one for our 'beef' and the other for our 'pork' " may be properly understood in this perspective (*vide* annexure I). Under such circumstances, we may safely conclude that the fear expressed by the Nagas signing the memorandum about the loss of their land or interference in their customs and usages, was not based on their own experience. The myth of hatred (for the Nagas) and their exploitation (by the Assamese/Indians) was created by the fertile colonial mind of the British Deputy Commissioner and a part of the British initiated propaganda.

The reasons to believe that the British Deputy Commissioner of Naga Hills district authored the above-mentioned document are the following:

1. The Naga identity was not fully established by that time, which the signatories themselves acknowledge.
2. There is no historical basis to assume that fears and apprehensions expressed in that document were based on the experience of the community.
3. The British did precious little to develop Naga Hills district; they did practically nothing for the well being of the Naga common man, and yet the document is full of the appreciation for them.
4. The Nagas who fought bitter battles against the British were not supposed to forget all that so soon without any valid reason.
5. All the signatories of the document were the British Government employees and therefore the direct beneficiaries of the British Raj. Reid, Hutton and Coupland wanted the hills to be separated from India and Burma before Independence. The British isolated Nagas from the rest of the country even prior to that.
6. The British officers, especially those serving in the North-East did not hide their dislike for the Hindus and the

Muslims. The document carries the same sentiment when it brings beef and pork in focus.

7. The common man in the Naga Hills district continued to be in favour of remaining in India. The Naga National Council resolution of 1946 wanted Naga Hills district to remain in Assam Province in India.

The Statehood was achieved by the Naga leaders having the backing of substantial Naga population. It is significant that almost one per cent of the population of Nagaland attended the three Naga People's Conventions. The people voted in large numbers disobeying the dictates of the underground Nagas. But the Union Territory status and the statehood was granted in a hurry. The moderate leaders should have waited and taken the underground Naga brothers with them. But they were in a hurry and had no patience even to wait for three years Interim Period. The President, Dr. Radhakrishnan inaugurated the State of Nagaland on 1st December, 1963. It was much before the stipulated time. The interim arrangements came to an end and the full-fledged State came into being. The dialogue between Mr. P. Shilu Ao, the then Chief Executive Councillor, and the Prime Minister Nehru on the subject of ending the Interim Period reveals an interesting fact. It goes as follows[13]:

Nehru: The Interim Period is for three years?

Shilu Ao: Your gesture to end it much before the time will be well received.

Nehru: But the violence continues and the hostiles are untractable.

Shilu Ao: Leave it to us to deal with our own kith and kin. I will request you to inaugurate the State.

Nehru: I shall send our philosopher-statesman to inaugurate the State. He is a holy soul. His blessing shall bring peace and amity.

Did the leaders, who brought Statehood, really tried, and in reality, had the capacity, to deal with their "own kith and kin?" The situation would have drastically changed if (*i*) the benefits of the huge fund pumped from Delhi was to deliver good at the lowermost level, and (*ii*) the on-going propaganda by the secessionists was effectively countered. After all the strength of the propaganda lies in the fact that these are never countered by anyone. The Nagas were made to believe that the Statehood was granted due to Delhi's fear of the gun and brought by the Underground. The signal that the "Violence pays" was never countered. It had many takers. "The Naga disturbances are unique in having an almost entirely political foundation."[14] On-going misinformation campaigns and propaganda keeps the issue alive.

Continuing Misinformations and the Propaganda

It is unfortunate that the media and intellectuals often talk on the Naga problem without properly confirming the facts. This creates confusion and complicates the issue, I will cite one such case and end the paper.

In a recently held seminar at Kohima, a Naga teacher of a Central University said: "the Sixteen-Point Agreement, signed between the Government of India and the Nagas, in sixties contains a clause which envisages merger of Naga dominated areas of adjoining states with Nagaland. Accordingly, Tuensang area of the then NEFA was merged with Nagaland. The Government of India should not go back on its commitment and should take necessary and immediate steps to integrate the Naga dominated areas of Manipur, Assam and Arunachal Pradesh with Nagaland."[15]

Some of the factual errors in the above-mentioned statement need correction:

1. There is nothing like Sixteen-Point Agreement, about which the scholar refers. In reality, it was the "Sixteen-Point Proposals" by the Naga People's Conference, submitted on 26 July, 1960, to Jawaharlal Nehru, the Prime Minister of India, by the Naga delegation. The Government of India accepted most of the proposals, but not all.
2. Tuensang was not merged with Nagaland as a result of the so-called Sixteen-Point Agreement. It was merged earlier with Naga Hills district of Assam to form Naga Hills Tuensang Area (NHTA), which was rechristened as Nagaland after the State formation.
3. It is not true that the Government of India made any

'commitment' to 'integrate the Naga dominated areas of Manipur, Assam, and Arunachal Pradesh with Nagaland'. The clause referring to the subject (Number 13; under the head **Consolidation of Contiguous Naga Areas)** reads: 'The delegation wished the following to be placed on record: "The Naga leaders expressed the view that other Naga inhabiting contiguous areas should be enabled to join the new State. It was pointed out to them on behalf of the Government of India that Articles 3 and 4 of the Constitution provided for increasing the area of any State, but that it was not possible for the Government of India to make any commitment in this regard at this stage." '

Thus it is amply clear that there was no agreement between the Government of India and the Naga delegation about the merger of the contiguous Naga areas. Here, it may be mentioned that the above-mentioned statement of the University teacher is not the only one of its kind. Such statements are often given by many persons giving the impression that Government of India has promised something, which is yet to be fulfilled.

REFERENCES

1. Prakash Singh, cited in *Nagaland*, p. 84.
2. S.K. Pillai, Faultline; p. 53; quoted from Ramuny, *The World of Nagas*.
3. Bareh, *Nagaland District Gazetteer, Kohima District*, p. 20.
4. See Annexure I.
5. Woodthorpe, cited in Elwin's *Nagas in the Nineteenth Century*, p. 47.
6. Gait, Sir Edward, *The History of Assam*, p. 308.
7. Gait, *op. cit.*, p. 79.
8. J.P. Mills, *The Ao Nagas*, p. 5.
9. *Ibid.*, pp. 11-12.
10. See the chapter on "Nagas: the Pre-British History".
11. A section of Changs do not take beef. Pork is taboo for the Marings.
12. See *People of India* by Kumar Suresh Singh.
13. Cited by Hokishe Sema, in *Emergence of Nagaland*, p. 96
14. Verrier Elwin, *Nagaland*, Shillong (1961), p. 70.
15. Paper presented by Dr. Xavier P. Mao, Department of Philosophy, North-Eastern Hill University, Shillong in the Seminar held by Centre for Democracy and Tribal Studies on 11 April, 2003 at Kohima on "Foundations of Naga Peoplehood: Roadmaps", proceedings, p. 34.

15

NAGALAND : THE ON-GOING STRIFE

The on-going strife in Nagaland reminds us of the following facts:

1. The understanding and the only accord, the Shillong Accord, have failed to bring the desired result.
2. The grant of statehood in two jumps in haste was a blunder; it has failed to solve the problem in the state and created problems elsewhere.
3. In spite of huge funding from the Central Government, the state has not developed to the desired level. Bigger states have been replicated in Nagaland. The large government machinery consumes enormous resources. There is also leakage of resources. Central and State Governments have failed to prevent flow of development funds to the coffers of the secessionist groups.
4. The State and Central Governments, in no time, succeeded in countering the myths and the propaganda of the terrorist groups. Media, knowingly or unknowingly, helped their cause. Politicisation of ethnicity owes its origin and growth mainly to propaganda and myth-making.
5. Lack of intellectual input in solving national problems, including the Naga Problem, is a well-known phenomenon. This is in spite of more than half a dozen Central Universities and institutes in the region, including one in Nagaland. Even an apex student body, like Naga Students Federation, bans research, is the indicator of the intellectual ethos generated by them.

The first Naga People's Convention held in 1957 was the most representative and the biggest in the history of the Naga till that date. More than one per cent of their population attended that Convention. They wanted Centrally Administered territory status for the area comprising of Naga Hills and Tuensang. It was granted and the Naga Hills Tuensang Area came into existence. Two more Naga People's Conventions were called soon after. They updated their demand and asked for full-fledged state. The new demand was also conceded; Nehru conceded and announced the formation of Nagaland as the 16th State of the Indian Union. An Interim Body with 45 members and 5-member Executive Council was formed for three years. The new power elite should have worked hard during the three years interim period to bring reconciliation, which they did not do. They were in a hurry, had no patience even to wait for that period and wanted the state to be inaugurated earlier. When Nehru reminded them of the three-year interim period, Shilu Ao, the Chief Executive Councillor said: "Your gesture to end it much before the time will be well-received." Nehru reminded them about the continuing violence and hostile situation. The reply was: "Leave it to us to deal with our own kith and kin."

As desired by them, the State was inaugurated before expiry of the interim period. Elections were held soon after. There was high percentage of voting. People ignored the boycott call given by the insurgents. This democratic factor, showing overwhelming public support for the statehood is always ignored by a section of the media, intellectuals and the secessionists.

The Nagas quickly updated their demands and got their Statehood. But were they satisfied? Mr. Kevichusa, a very senior Naga leader and former bureaucrat, addressing a well attended public meeting convened to welcome the Peace Mission members at Kohima in April 1964, made a strong plea to 'start all over again'. He wanted dissolution of the newly elected Legislative Assembly and doing away with the ministry. A section of the Nagas wanted Sikkim status in 1965. The quick succession of the demands which were met immediately affected the Naga phyche. A large section of the Nagas believe in the propaganda that 'Statehood was granted due to the fear of the Naga gun'; that 'the Nagaland was formed due to Phizo and not due to Nehru's real concern for the Naga people. The myths like

'Delhi fears', 'the flow of money shall stop or be partially retarded, if peace comes, have wide currency. The Centre is blamed for giving fund and making them corrupt. Centre is also blamed for providing inadequate fund and keeping them under-developed. Even educated and conscientious persons very comfortably talk 'to teach Delhi a lesson'.

India's successful and pleasant interface with Asia amply proves that its attitude was never racial. The country's value system was never coloured by the consideration of race and colour. Communication gap between the people of a vast country like India can, naturally, not be avoided. Even educated Nagas fail to name all the Naga tribes. Americans confuse between bearded Arabs and Sikhs. But a Naga for any of the countrymen is never "non-Indian-looking" and without good Indian name. Such distorted perceptions are of the Nagas own making. Charles Chasie is a highly intelligent Naga journalist and a person with extensive exposure. He alleges that the attitude of the Indian leadership towards the Nagas starting from the initial "wooing" with Nehru and others, so tragically metamorphosed several times and went on to one of patronization, indifference, deviousness and outright arrogance, even insult. Charles Chasie is not alone in levelling such allegations, which have no basis. The continuing problem has made complex situation and mindset.

The Naga problem continues to defy solution and there is no hope that the problem will be solved soon. However sincere effort should continue towards resolving the conflict. The Statehood was granted to the Nagas in a hurry without waiting for obtaining widest consensus. Such mistake should never be committed in future. Nationalist Socialist Council of Nagalim—Isak-Muiva (NSCN-IM) is the strongest militant group in Nagaland. The other faction is NSCN-K, whose leader is S.S. (Robert) Khaplang. The two NSCN factions have the military punch with about 4,000 and 1,000 weapons respectively. There were two factions of the Naga National Council (NNC). One faction of NNC has merged with NSCN-IM. The only remaining faction, NNC(Adino) is comparatively weak. There a cease-fire agreement between the Centre and the NSCN-IM since 1997. The cease-fire agreement between the Centre and NSCN-K was also signed in 2002. These agreements have brought relative peace in Nagaland. But the forcible conversion continues in

Tirap and Changlang districts of Arunachal Pradesh, which is not a good development. Th. Muivah the leader of NSCN-IM is a Tangkhul Naga from Manipur. S.S. Khaplang is Heimi Naga from Myanmar. The Heimis are a cognate tribe of the Konyak Nagas of India. Both the factions have vested interest in greater Nagaland. It needs mention that the cease-fire agreement with NSCN-K in 2001 was not liked by NSCN-IM, as it insisted on being recognized as the sole representative of the Naga people. It, however, tolerated the development. The two factions had sustained internecine conflict with each other. Out of the total insurgency related killings of 376 during three and half years of cease-fire between August 1, 1997 and January 31, 2001, as many as 236 were killed in their factional warfare.

Inconsistency is a marked phenomenon related to Naga problem. At the same time "traitor" is a very cheap word which is liberally used. The Naga National Council (NNC) passes a resolution just before independence according to which they wanted Naga Hills district to remain a district of Assam in free India. Very soon, NNC reversed its stand, and wanted Nagas to secede from India. The opposition to the secessionist group continued strong even within the Naga National Council for some time and Phizo had to leave NNC and form People' Independence League. But he captured NNC after "Naga Council—Hydari Understanding" fiasco. The NNC signed Shillong Accord in 1975 and the NNC and the Naga Federal Government accepted the Constitution of India. But a splinter group revived the old demands of Naga Sovereignty. Th. Muivah and S.S. Khaplang formed Nationalist Socialist Council of Nagalim in 1980. They, afterwards split the organization into two factions in 1988.

Creation of Nagaland State, as mentioned earlier, and that too without a wide-ranging consensus, was a blunder. Even the conscientious Naga opinion agrees to the same. It did not solve the problem; at the same time, it created problems elsewhere. The entire North-East has been destabilized. There were numerous Small State demands. Viability ceased to be a criteria. People got the wrong signal that 'Violence pays'. Nagaland was replicated elsewhere, as for example, in Mizoram. Of course, Mizoram Accord was a success, whereas, all the accords/understandings with the Nagas registered failures. Substantial funds came in the trail of Statehood to Nagaland. It was used for creating huge government machinery, which consumed most of the resources. Again, there was pilferage. Precious little was left for revenue earning productive expenditure. Even insurgency was funded by the funds flowing from Delhi.

The flow of huge fund in Nagaland created a relatively resource-rich area in Nagaland and resource-poor areas in its neighbourhood. This fector, along with Nagaland Statehood, created a "sense of grievance" in the North-East, especially in Manipur. The fear of transfer of Ukhrul, Tamenglong, Senapati and Chandel districts from Manipur to Nagaland in the light of the NSCN-IM's demand of greater Nagalim has, therefore, heightened their sense of grievance and fear. The popular resentment, leading to unprecedented public protest over the extension of the area of cease-fire of the June 14, 2001 agreement of the Government of India with NSCN-IM, leading to the revocation of the three words—"without territorial limits"—from clause 1 of the said agreement by the former was the expression of the same.

The NSCN(IM) strategy is to keep mounting pressure on the Government of India for a greater Nagaland. It wants to be the main arbiter of the final settlement and hopes to tire out Government of India in conceding this. The organization has acquired a definite clout in the State after the last election in which it resorted to extensive coercion and is now engaged in silencing any opposition to it. Extortion and coercion are increasing and are likely to distort the democratic process itself in the state. NSCN(IM) is going to get emboldened and more demanding. It plans to turn the history of the region on its head through its demands and keep the regional tension alive as a tactics.

Nagas very often talk about the political solution on the problem. But none of them spell out its parameters in specific terms. Many, when talking about "final statement of the Naga political problem", vaguely think of something higher than the statehood. Unfortunately, crossing the thresholds of the present parameters of the Statehood shall lead to similar demands from many other corners and is difficult to concede. The present difficulty with the Naga problem is due to (*i*) lack of consensus among the Nagas, especially among the insurgent outfits, and (*ii*) difficulty in meeting the demands of the greater Nagalim, made by NSCN-IM.

Muivah, the powerful leader of NSCN-IM dose not believe in consensus. He is arrogant and dictatorial. His two visits to the Communist China militated against grassroot Naga democracy more than any other factor. Any settlement with him without wide ranging consensus among the Nagas is sure to meet the same fate as creation of Nagaland State (1964) with the NNO; and that of the Shillong accord (1975) with the NNC. Others will not accept it as final. The NSCN-IM almost succeeded in this battle of nerves when the Government of India unwittingly agreed to extend the cease-fire (2002) to all the "claimed" Naga inhabited areas, but retrieved in time. It reflected a mind-set among the negotiators which NSCN-IM is trying to exploit. The agitation against the extension of cease-fire area in the North-East, and especially in Manipur, have amply proved that any concession on greater Nagaland will open a Pandora's box which will be difficult to contain and control. Such a move will neither be practical nor historically correct.

The Nagas also demand the merger of the Naga inhabited areas of Myanmar to form greater Nagaland. They forget that the passing of the national boundaries through ethnic regions dividing the communities between the nations is a global phenomenon. It happened due to European colonialism. Any attempt to interfere with national boundaries shall lead to wars at global levels between the nations and the world community shall never allow the same.

At present there is no consensus among different insurgent outfits of the Nagas. Naga Hoho was trying to built up a consensus and as "facilitators". But it has been thrown out by the NSCN-IM. The facilitators were termed "traitors" and "agents". The work of healing has become difficult. However, even if there is consensus, a demand is made and met; there is least possibility of peace in the state. Conceding more will satisfy some or all the insurgent groups, but there is no guarantee that a splinter group may not revive the problem, keep it alive, progress inch by inch. In anyway, it will be counter-productive; the struggle will not cease by *ad hoc* measures and conceding one after another.

The Nagas are excellent at documentation; they pick up things from here and there and use them. Their brinkmanship and strong element of mind helps in the same. Gandhi did not talk to the Naga delegation only about the "freedom of the Nagas". He also talked about the "freedom of the Bhangi colony". The Nagas talked about the former without linking it with the latter. It is as good as misquoting Gandhi. The Governor of a state, like Akbar Hydari, was supposed to know his brief and legal capacity. The controversial articles of understanding with Akbar Hydari should be explained keeping this fact in mind. Again over-publicised plebiscite was not properly conducted and it represented the view of a limited section of the Nagas only. There are gaps in the understanding of the problem which the country is facing in the Nagaland and rest of the North-East. It needs intellectual input and sincere handling. The issue in the North-East in one state is interlinked with issues in other states.

There should not only be fiscal input, but proper utilization of the same. Its benefits should percolate to the grassroots level. Centre and the institutions of learning should endeavour to bring change in the system of education. Atleast Central Universities and the IITs of the region should develop into centres of excellence.

The on-going strife get strength and sustenance due to system's internal weaknesses as all as external factors. As the state fails to deliver, common man fail to receive their share of benefit, thereby extortion has become a way of sharing. Appropriation of the development benefits by a section of the society results in alienation and the related ailments. Examples are not lacking when there is close collusion between insurgent forces and the duly elected civil governments. The insurgent outfits of the North-East get support from ISI, Bangladesh and China; have camps in Bangladesh, Myanmar and Bhutan. ULFA and Bodo insurgents became weak when Bhutanese Army acted to force them to remove their camps from Southern Bhutan. NSCN-K offer for talks came after joint Indo-Myanmar intervention against their camps in Myanmar. However, it is foolish to expect such things either from ISI or Bangladesh in near future due to obvious reason. The support net-work of NSCN-IM is very strong. The organization's net-working with the terrorist outfits of India and abroad is well-known. This makes the organization strong. NSCN, like other insurgent outfits of the North-East, derives strength by raising emotive issues. It indulges into misleading propaganda and takes the advantage of the simplicity and ignorance of the people. People are often silenced by creating terror. The situation, anyway, demands mature handling. Delhi cannot indefinitely act in the mechanical way and allow the situation to worsen.

ANNEXURES

ANNEXURE-I

MEMORANDOM OF THE NAGA HILLS TO SIMON COMMISSION

(JANUARY 10, 1929)

Sir,

We the undersigned Nagas of the Naga Club at Kohima who are the only persons at present who can voice for our people have heard with great regret that our Hills were included within the Reformed Scheme of India without our knowledge, but as the administration of our Hills continued to be in the hands of the British Officers we did not consider it necessary to raise any protest in the past. Now, we learn that you have come to India as representatives of the British Government to enquire into the working of the system of Government and the growth of the Education and we beg to submit our view with the prayer that our Hills may be withdrawn from the Reformed Schemes and placed outside the Reforms but directly under the British Government. We never asked for any reforms and we do not wish any reforms.

Before the British Government conquered our country in 1879-80, we were living in a state of intermittent warfare with the Assamese of the Assam valley to the North and West of our country and Manipuris in the South. They never conquered us nor were we subjected to their rule. On the other hand, we were always a terror to these people. Our country within the administered area consists of more than eight Tribes, quite different from one another with quite different languages which cannot be understood by each other, and there are more Tribes outside the administered area which are not known at present. We have no unity among us and it is really the British Government that is holding us together now.

Our education at present is poor, the occupation of our country by the British Government being so recent as 1880, we have had no chances or opportunity to improve in Education and though we can boast of two or three graduates of an Indian University in our country, we have not got one yet who is able to represent all our different tribes or master our language, much less, one to represent us in any Council or Province. Moreover, our population numbering 1,02,000 is very small in comparison with the population of the plains districts in the Province, and any representation that may be allotted to us in the Council will be negligible and will carry no weight whatsoever. Our language is quite different from those of the plains and we have no social affinities with Hindus or Muslims. We are looked down upon by the one for our 'beef' and the other for our 'pork' and by both for our want in Education which is not due to any fault of ours.

Our country is poor and it does not pay for it administrations. Therefore, if it is continued to be placed under the Reformed Scheme, we are afraid, that new and heavy taxes will have to be imposed on us and when we cannot pay them all our land will have to be sold and in the long run, we shall have no share in the land of our birth and life will not be worth living then. Though our land at present is within the British Territory, Government has always recognised our private rights in it. But if we are forced to enter the Council of the majority all these rights may be extinguished by an unsympathetic Council, the majority of whose number is sure to belong to the Plain Districts. We also have much fear the introduction of foreign laws and customs to supersede our own customary laws which we now enjoy.

For the above reasons, we pray that the British Government will continue to safeguard our rights against all encroachment from other people who are more advanced than us by withdrawing our country from the Reformed Scheme and placing it directly under its own protection. If the British Government, however, wants to throw us away, we pray that we should not be thrust to the mercy of the people who could never subjugate us, but to leave us alone to determine for ourselves as in ancient times. We claim to represent all those tribes to which we belong—Angamis, Kacha Nagas, Kukis, Semas, Lothas, and Rengmas.

Yours faithfully,

1. I Nihu, Head Interpreter, Angami
2. Nisalie, Peshkar, Angami
3. Nisier, Master, Angami
4. Khosa, Doctor, Angami
5. Gepo, Interpreter, Kacha Naga
6. Vipunyti, Potdar, Angami
7. Goyiepra, Treasurer, Angami
8. Ruzhukhrie, Master, Angami
9. Dikhrie, Sub-Overseer, Angami
10. Zapuchulie, Master, Angami
11. Zepulie, Interpreter, Angami
12. Katsumo, Interpreter, Angami
13. Nuolhoukielie, Clerk, Angami
14. Luzevi, Interpreter, Sema,
15. Apamo, Interpreter, Lotha
16. Resilo, Interpreter, Rengma
17. Lengjang, Interpreter, Kuki
18. Nikhriehu, Interpreter, Angami
19. Miakra-o, Chaprasi, Angami
20. Levi, Clerk, Kacha Naga

ANNEXURE-II

NINE-POINT UNDERSTANDING

Tribes Represented at Discussions on 25, 27 and 28 June, 1947, at Kohima

Western Angamis
Eastern Angamis
Kukis
Kacha Nagas (Nzemi)
Rengmas
Semas
Lothas
Aos
Sangtams
Changs

Head of Proposed Understanding

That the right of the Nagas to develop themselves according to their freely expressed wishes is recognized.

1. *Judicial:* All cases whether civil or criminal arising between Nagas in the Naga Hills will be disposed of by duly constituted Naga Courts according to Naga customary law or such as may be introduced with the consent of duly recognized Naga representative organizations: save that where a sentence of transportation or death has been passed there will be a right of appeal to the Governor.

   In cases arising between Nagas and non-Nagas in

   (*a*) Kohima and Mokokchung town areas, and

   (*b*) In the neighbouring plains districts, the judge, if not a Naga, will be assisted by a Naga assessor.

2. *Executive:* The general principle is accepted that what the Naga Council is prepared to pay for, the Naga Council should control. This principle will apply equally to the work done as well as the staff employed.

While the District Officer will be appointed at the discretion of the Governor, Subdivisions of the Naga Hills should be administered by a Subdivisional Council with a full-time executive President paid by the Naga Council who would be responsible to the District Officer for all matters falling within the latter's responsibility, and to the Naga Council for all matters falling within their responsibility.

In regard to:

(*a*) Agriculture—The Naga Council will exercise all the powers now vested in the District Officer.

(*b*) CWD—The Naga Council would take over full control.

(*c*) Eduation and Forest Department—The Naga Council is prepared to pay for all the services and staff.

3. *Legislative:* That no laws passed by the Provincial or Central Legislature which would materially affect the terms of this agreement or the religious practices of the Nagas shall have legal force in the Naga Hills without the consent of the Naga Council. In cases of dispute as to whether any law did so affect this agreement the matter would be referred by the Naga Council to the Governor who would then direct that the law in question should not have legal force in the Naga Hills pending the decision of the Central Government.

4. *Land:* That land with all its resources in the Naga Hills should not be alienated to a non-Naga without the consent of the Naga Council.

5. *Taxation:* That the Naga-Council will be responsible for the imposition, collection, and expenditure of land revenue and house tax and of such other taxes as may be imposed by the Naga Council.

6. *Boundaries:* That present administrative divisions should be modified so as:

(*i*) to bring back into the Naga Hills district all the forests transferred to the Sibsagar and Nowgong districts in the past, and

(*ii*) to bring under one unified administrative unit as far as possible all Nagas. All the areas so included would be within the scope of the present proposed agreement. No areas should be transferred out of the Naga Hills without the consent of the Naga Council.

7. *Arms Act:* The Deputy Commissioner will act on the advice of the Naga Council in accordance with the provisions of the Arms Act.
8. *Regulations:* The Chin Hills Regulations and the Bengal Eastern Frontier Regulations will remain in force.
9. *Period of Agreement:* The Governor of Assam as the Agent of the Government of the Indian Union will have a special responsibility for a period of 10 years to ensure the due observance of this agreement, at the end of this period the Naga Council will be asked whether they require the above agreement to be extended for a further period or a new agreement regarding the future of the Naga people arrived at.

ANNEXURE-III

SIXTEEN-POINT PROPOSALS

The points placed by the delegates of the Naga People's Convention before the Prime Minister on 26 July 1960 as finally recast by the delegation in the light of discussions on 27 and 28 July, 1960 with the Foreign Secretary.

1. The Name

The territories that were heretofore known as the Naga Hills-Tuensang Area under the Naga Hills-Tuensang Area Act, 1957, shall form a State within the Indian Union and be hereafter known as Nagaland.

2. The Ministry In-charge

The Nagaland shall be under Ministry of External Affairs of the Government of India.

3. The Governor for Nagaland

(*a*) The President of India shall appoint a Governor for Nagaland and he will be vested with executive powers of the Government of Nagaland. He will have his headquarters in Nagaland.

(*b*) His administrative secretariat will be headed by Chief Secretary stationed at the headquarters with other secretariat staff as necessary.

(*c*) The Governor shall have special responsibility with regard to law and order during transitional period and for so long as the law and order situation continues to remain disturbed on account of hostile activities. In exercising this special responsibility, the Governor shall, after consultation with the Ministry, act in his individual judgement. This special responsibility of the Governor will cease when normalcy returns.

4. Council of Ministers

(*a*) There shall be a Council of Ministers with a Chief Minister at the head to assist and advise the Governor in the exercise of his functions.

(*b*) The Council of Ministers shall be responsible to the Naga Legislative Assembly.

5. The Naga Legislature

There shall be constituted a Legislative Assembly consisting of elected and nominated members as may be deemed necessary representing different tribes. (Further, a duly constituted body of Experts may be formed to examine and determine the principles of representation on democratice basis.)

6. Representation in the Parliament

Two elected members shall represent Nagaland in the Union Parliament, that is to say, one for the Lok Sabha and the other for the Rajya Sabha.

7. Acts of Parliament

"No Acts or Law passed by the Union Parliament affecting the following provisions shall have legal force in Nagaland unless specially applied to it by the majority vote of the Naga Legislative Assembly."

(*a*) The Religious or Social practices of the Nagas.

(*b*) Naga Customary Laws and Procedure.

(*c*) Civil and criminal justice so far as these concern decisions according to Naga Customary Laws. The existing laws relating to administration of civil and criminal justice as provided in the Rules for the Administration of Justice and Police in the Naga Hills district shall continue to be in force.

(*d*) The ownership and transfer of land and its resources.

8. Local Self Government

Each tribe shall have the following units of rule-making and administrative local bodies to deal with matters concerning the respective tribes and areas:

(*a*) The Village Council.

(*b*) The Range Council.

(*c*) The Tribal Council.

These Councils will also deal with disputes and cases involving breaches of customary laws and usages.

9. Administrative of Justice

(*a*) The existing system of administration of civil and crimina justice shall continue.

(*b*) Appelate Courts:

(*i*) The District Court-cum-Sessions Court (for each district), High Court and Supreme Court of India.

(*ii*) The Naga Tribunal (for the whole of the Nagaland) in respect of cases decided according to Customary Law.

10. Administrative of Tuensang District

(*a*) The Governor shall carry on the administration of the Tuensang district for a period of 10 (ten) years until such time when the tribes in the Tuensang district are capable of shouldering more responsibilities of the advance system of administration. The commencement of the ten years period of administration will start simultaneously with enforcement of detailed workings of Constitution in other parts of the Nagaland.

(*b*) Provided further that a Regional Council shall be formed for Tuensang district by elected representatives from all the tribes in Tuensang district, and the Governor may nominate representatives to the Regional Council as well. The Deputy Commissioner will be the *ex-officio* Chairman of the Council. The Regional Council will elect members to the Naga Legislative Assembly to represent Tuensang district.

(*c*) Provided further that on the advice of the Regional Council, steps will be taken to start various councils and courts in those areas where the people feel themselves capable of establishing such institutions.

(*d*) Provided further that no Act or Law passed by the Naga Legislative Assembly shall be applicable to Tuensang district unless specifically recommended by the Regional Council.

(*e*) Provided further that the Regional Council shall supervise and guide the working of the various Councils and Tribal Courts within Tuensang district and wherever necessary depute the local officers to act as Chairman thereof.

(*f*) Provided further that Councils of such areas inhabited by a mixed population or which have not as yet decided to which specific tribal Council to be affiliated to, shall be directly under the Regional Councils for the time being.

And at the end of ten years the situation will be reviewed and if the people so desired the period will be further extended.

11. Financial Assistance from Government of India

To supplement the revenues of the Nagaland, there will be need for the Government of India to pay out of the Consolidated Fund of India.

(*a*) A lumpsum each year for the development programme in the Nagaland, and

(*b*) A grant-in-aid towards meeting the cost of administration.

Proposals for the above grants shall be prepared and submitted by the Government of Nagaland to the Government of India for their approval. The Governor will have general responsibility for ensuring that the funds made available by the Government of India are expended for the purpose for which they have been approved.

12. Re-transfer of Reserved Forests

The delegation wished the following to be placed on record:

"The Naga delegation discussed the question of the inclusion of the Reserve Forests and of contiguous areas inhabited by the Nagas. They were referred to the provisions in Articles 3 and 4 of the Constitution, prescribing the procedure for the transfer of area from one State to another."

13. Consolidation of Contiguous Naga Areas

The delegation wished the following to be placed on record: "The Naga leaders expressed the view that other Naga inhabiting contiguous areas should be enabled to join the new State. It was pointed out to them on behalf of the Government of India that Articles 3 and 4 of the Constitution provided for increasing the area of any State, but that it was not possible for the Government of India to make any commitment in this regard at this stage."

14. Formation of Separate Naga Regiment

In order that the Naga people can fulfil their desire of playing a full role in the defence forces of India, the question of raising a separate Naga Regiment should be duly examined for action.

15. Transitional Period

(*a*) On reaching the political settlement with the Government of India, the Government of India with prepare a Bill for such amendment of the Constitution, as may be necessary, in order to implement the decisions; draft Bill, before presentation to Parliament, will be shown to the delegates of the NPC.

(*b*) There shall be constituted an Interim Body with elected repreventatives from every tribe to assist and advise the Governor in the Administration of the Nagaland during the transitional period. The tenure of office of the members of the Interim Body will be 3 (three) years subject to re-election.

16. Inner Line Regulation

Rules embodied in the Bengal Eastern Frontier Regulation, 1873 shall remain in force in the Nagaland.

Sd/- Dr. Imkongliba Ao
President

INDEX